THE PAPERBACK FANTASTIC VOLUME THREE
Published August 2022

EDITED
by Justin Marriott (thepaperbackfanatic@sky.com)

ASSISTANT EDITOR
Tom Tesarek

COVER DESIGNED
by Bill Cunningham (cinexploits@gmail.com)
Front cover image from *The Drums of Dracula*. Artist unknown
Frontispiece from **Twisted Tales 6**, art by John Bolton
All art and images reproduced purely for the purposes of historical context and no copyright infringement intended

CONTRIBUTORS
Steve Carroll
S Clayton Rhodes
James Doig
Ian Millsted
Roy Nugen
John Peel
Jeff Popple
Scott Ranalli
Penny Tesarek
Tom Tesarek
Benjamin Thomas

THE PAPERBACK FANTASTIC

VOLUME 3

HORROR

The Paperback Fantastic – Reviews Listing

The Ants	6
The Apocalypse	6
The Beetle	6
Blood of My Blood	8
Books of Blood Volume Four	8
Carrion Comfort	11
The Ceremonies	11
Children of the Night	12
The Conjurers	12
Contents for Sale	17
A Corben Special	17
The Degenerates	17
The Demon	18
Devil Daddy	18
Doctors Wear Scarlet	21
The Dogs	21
Draco the Dragon Man	22
The Dreamers	22
The Evil Under the Water	27
The 16th Fontana Book of Great Horror Stories	27
Frankenstein's Tread	27
Ghost Rider	29
Headhunter	29
Homonculus	32
The Horror in the Heights	32
The Horror Stories of Robert E Howard	32
House on the Borderland	35
Invisible Men	35
The Island of Dr Moreau	35
Killer Crabs	36
Manstopper	36
Maynard's House	36
The Nest	41
Night Shift	41
Nightshades and Damnations	42
An Odour of Decay	42

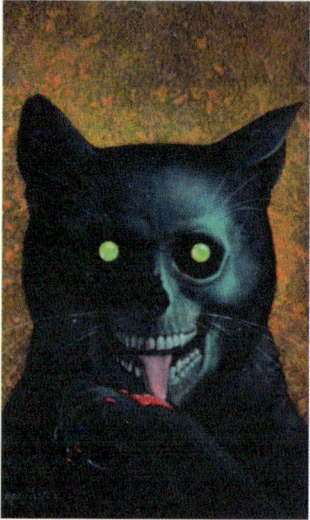

The Offspring	44
Razorback	44
Sabat	44
The Saxonbury Print Out	46
The Scarlet Boy	46
Seven Tickets to Hell	51
Shades of Evil	51
The Slime Beast	52
Some of your Blood	52
Tales of Love and Horror	52
Tapping the Vein volume one	55
To the Devil - a Daughter	55
Tomb of Dracula	59
Twilight Eyes	59
Twisted Tales	60
Two Fisted Zombies	60
Two Thousand Maniacs	62
The Unbidden	62
The Unholy Smile	62
Vampire$	64
Village of Blood	66
The Village of Fear	66
Whispers	66
The Wrath	70
Zacherley's Midnight Snacks	70
Zacherley's Vulture Stew	70

Fantastic Focus

Peter Tremayne	14
Signet on the Rampage	24
Frankenstein	30
Charles Birkin	38
The Satan Sleuth	48
Drac is Back!	56
Drakulon Lives!	68

THE ANTS
Peter Tremayne
1979

"Doesn't conform to the normal formula utilised in the 'animals attack' genre..."

At a time when UK publishers stampeded towards the "nasty" genre and made their books as squishy and oozy as possible, this title and others produced by Peter Beresford Ellis as Peter Tremayne across the 1980s, are on the milder side of horror. They hark back to earlier eras, reminding me of the UK Badger Books of the 60s (but written with more care and craft) or even the pulps of the 1930s. Certainly, *The Ants* had the feel of a jungle adventure story, with a pilot and anthropologist stranded in the Amazon falling in love whilst solving the challenge of repelling wave upon wave of flesh-eating soldier ants. There are welcome macabre touches early in the book, such as the discovery by the anthropologist of a huge pile of gleaming white human bones - which included the remains of her father - or the captain of a steam ship still clasping his wheel despite being stripped of all flesh by the ants from the waist down. But these are the exceptions rather than the rule, and the book doesn't conform to the normal formula utilised in the 'animals attack' genre to which this book is normally catalogued. The ants are neither giant nor possessed of an enhanced intelligence, despite the suggestion a US plane carrying atomic material crash-landing may have started the phenomenon of the ant's migration, and there isn't the conventional conveyor-belt of victims for the ants. I am sure that Beresford Ellis doesn't regard this as his finest work, and I can't recommend it as an especially notable example of the genre.

Justin Marriott

THE APOCALYPSE
Jeffrey Konvitz
1979

"Warmed-over scraps from its predecessor..."

A hugely disappointing follow up to his excellent *The Sentinel*, source of the controversial film by Michael Winner. The job from hell is about to become vacant, with the Catholic church looking for someone new to become blind, deaf, dumb and paralysed in order to sit in a New York apartment as the next sentinel, guarding against the presence of Satan. Part police-procedure thriller, part whodunit and part conspiracy pulp, *The Apocalypse* has a complex structure and lofty intentions but reads like warmed-over scraps from its predecessor and doesn't really warrant the effort. There were some belting twists at the end, but if I hadn't been reviewing it, I would have given up long before.

Justin Marriott

THE BEETLE
Richard Marsh
1897

"Dancing around the nature of the supernatural element..."

A classic horror story with a healthy dose of a detective/mystery element to it. Originally published in serial form under the name "The Peril of Paul Lessingham: The Story of a Haunted Man", it actually out-sold Bram Stoker's *Dracula*, published that same year. The plot involves an ancient Egyptian supernatural entity that tries to take revenge on a British Member of Parliament (Paul Lessingham) for an atrocity committed at a temple in Cairo some twenty years ago. The novel is broken down into four parts, each with its own first-person narrator who relate the events that happen over a three-day period. There are a few minor overlaps among their stories, just enough to show how they relate to one

---

THE ANTS US Signet edition from 1980, with cover art possibly by Tom Hallman who produced many of the Signet horror covers of that era.

THE BEETLE 1959 paperback edition from UK publishers World Distributors. Cover painted by Ron Smethurst who also produced a cover for their edition of *Turn of the Screw*, but mainly worked in their Xmas annuals tying in with TV series and personalities.

THE APOCALYPSE This sequel to the hit *The Sentinel* (1974) was known as *The Guardian* in America. David McAllister produced the well-designed art for this 1979 paperback from New English Library.

THE CLASSIC HORROR STORY OF OUR TIME
WDL BOOKS
THE BEETLE
RICHARD MARSH
3/6

THE APOCALYPSE
THE SHATTERING SEQUEL TO THE SENTINEL
BY JEFFREY KONVITZ

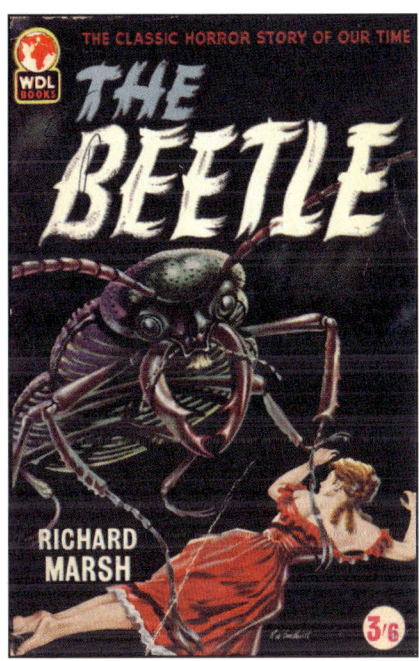

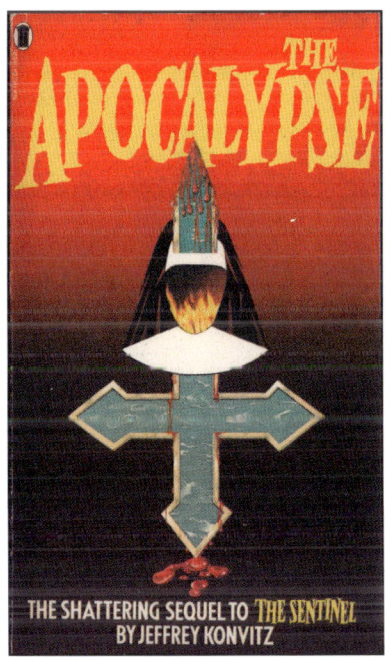

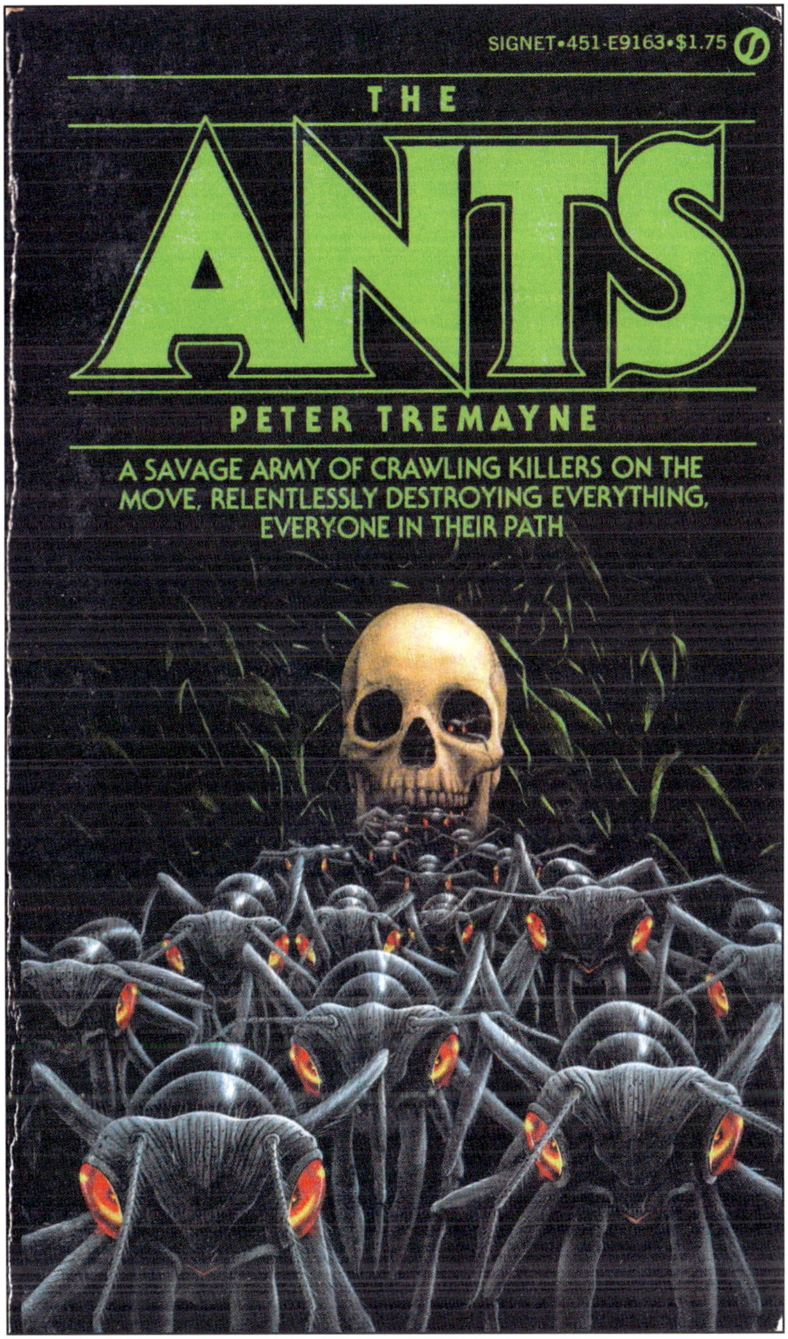
SIGNET•451-E9163•$1.75
THE
ANTS
PETER TREMAYNE
A SAVAGE ARMY OF CRAWLING KILLERS ON THE MOVE, RELENTLESSLY DESTROYING EVERYTHING, EVERYONE IN THEIR PATH

another, but for the most part, we get to hear about new facts of the case as experienced from their own personal point of view. Interestingly, the fourth and final narrator is a detective who is able to pull all the strings of the plot together and provide context as well as a conclusion to the strange events. The nature of the supernatural entity is not completely explained in the book. It appears to be a scarab beetle, quite a bit larger than normally found and has unusual abilities. There are also two Egyptian cult members who worship both Isis and the scarab entity although it is implied that both cultists are actually the same individual. I found the novel to be much better than I expected. It's fairly easy to read, unlike some fiction that was written during that era and the narrative plot was intriguing to be sure. It has a similar style to the original *Dracula*, meaning there is a lot of exposition as well as dancing around the nature of the supernatural element, leaving it more mysterious I suppose. Overall, a great classic read.

Benjamin Thomas

BLOOD OF MY BLOOD
Errol Lecale (Wilfried McNeilly)
1975

"The ultimate Hammer Horror movie never made..."

The sixth and final entry in **The Specialist** series, written by Wilfried McNeilly as Errol Lecale. McNeilly was a total pulp writer of the British Fleet Street variety. He wrote **Sexton Blake** and **The Guardians** series as Peter Saxon, which is him playing in the same occult wheelhouse, albeit a hip-60's-Mod version. What this really boils down to is a Boy's Own Adventure Story with two double-scoops of monster mayhem. Eli Podgram is the titular Specialist who, of course, isn't a podiatrist. There seemed to be quite a few of those occult-professionals in Victorian England. Opening on the final scene might have been a misstep, I got the impression that I was watching the final chapter in a cliff-hanger serial. But hell, I still enjoyed the whole thing. Podgram must travel to his ancestral home because a door got opened and to stop all the monsters who started a club with a nefarious plot to kill him. Along for the ride are two characters I found annoying, but I did like his mute sidekick, Mara. Then there's werewolves or were-cats, vampires, ghouls, spookiness, nights in Transylvania, stiff upper-lips, and shapeshifters. It's basically like the ultimate Hammer Horror movie never made. It might have moved a little too fast for its own good, I felt two steps behind the book at times, but I guess I might just need to read the first five to catch up.

Roy Nugen

BOOKS OF BLOOD VOLUME 4
Clive Barker
1985

"A metaphor for Barker's impact on British horror fiction..."

I read the *Books of Blood* upon publication but not since, so I returned in trepidation for fear of ruining the fond memories. My fears were unfounded, with all the stories being of a high quality and standing the test of time. I couldn't recollect any of the tales at first glance, but 'Revelations' set in a delightfully seedy Texas motel haunted by a couple whose ongoing disputes are heard by the bullied wife of a fire and brimstone preacher, soon flooded back as the stand-out in this volume. Another winner, 'The Age of Desire' with its scenes of a lab full of chimpanzees deliberately infected with rage, sorry, lust, made me wonder if Alex Garland, screenwriter of *28 Days Later* might have been reading Barker back in the day. The lead character, who has been infected with an insatiable sexual appetite, rampages around London's red-light district, gleefully spilling blood and semen as he comes and goes. I imagine this may have been Barker's own commentary on the self-consuming 'greed is good' philosophy of the 80s and the increasing use of sexual imagery in mainstream advertising and culture. I also think it could function as a metaphor for Barker and his own impact on British horror fiction, with his bravura imagination and celebration of diverse sexuality having a megaton-force impact on the repetitive and narrow-minded horror fiction of that period. Indeed, later sections of 'The Body Politic', where a sea of disembodied hands overwhelm a prison, were reminiscent of that mainstay of the 80s, the 'when-animals-attack genre. A bloody brilliant read, and worth cracking open the pages of the old copies you haven't revisited in years. The multi-talented Barker even did the covers for the editions on the opposite page. *Justin Marriott*

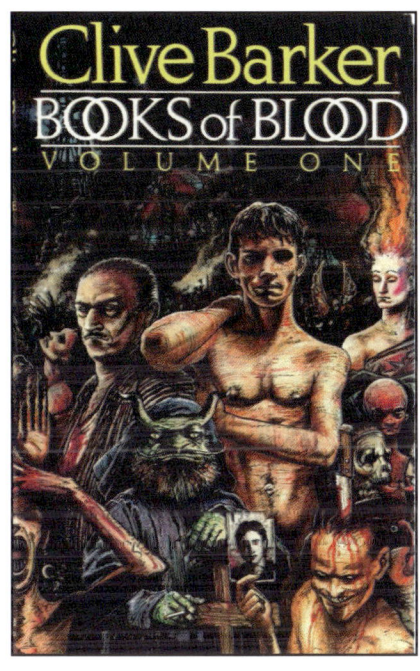
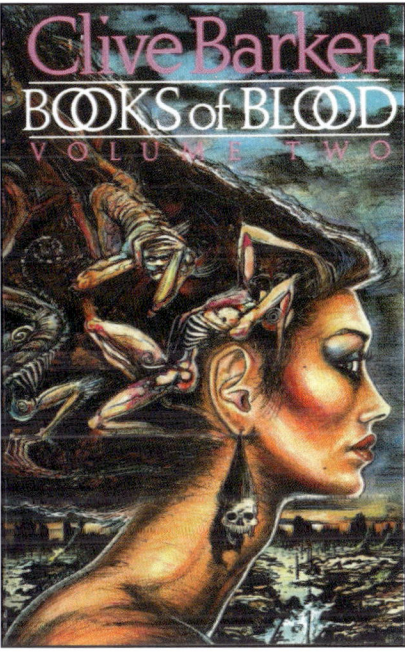

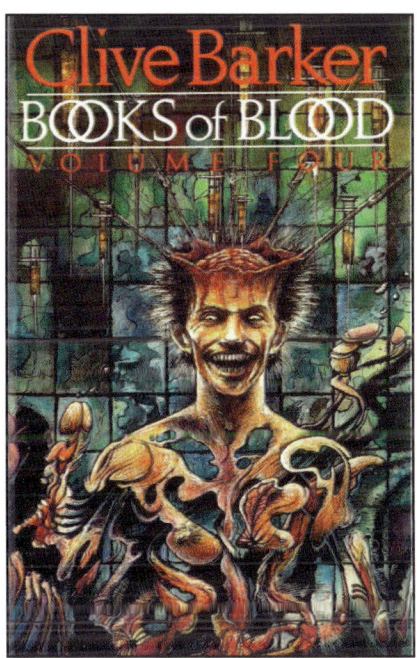

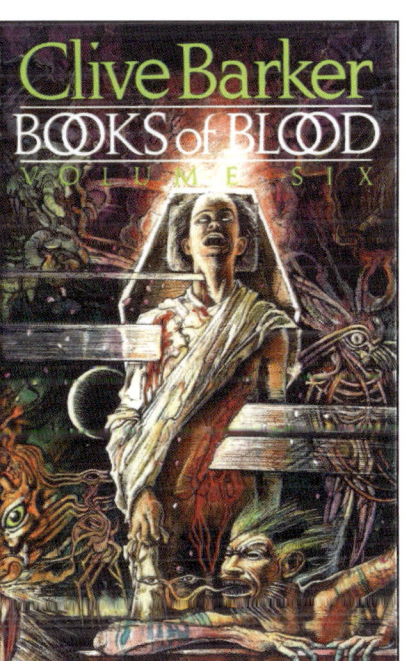

the PAPERBACK FANtastic – HORROR

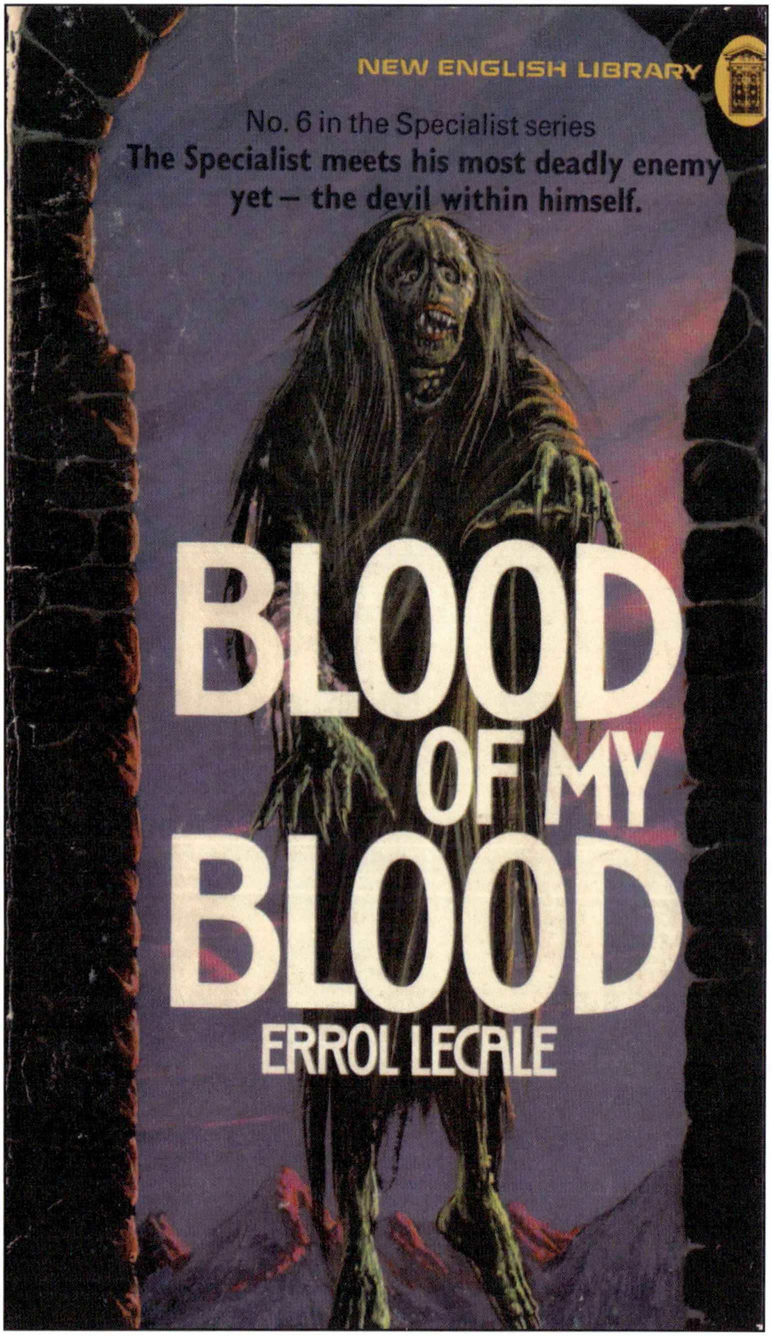

The Paperback Fantastic – Horror

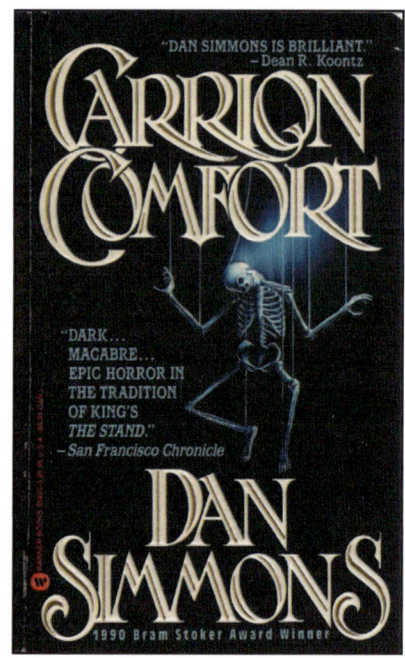

CARRION COMFORT
Dan Simmons
1989

"Perhaps the single best ending to a novel that I have personally ever read..."

Let's start this review with a qualifier: *Carrion Comfort* by Dan Simmons is easily one of my top 3 favourite horror novels of all time, even though it straddles multiple genres, including espionage, historical fiction, and revenge thriller. But make no mistake—this is ultimately a horror novel of the first magnitude. It won the Bram Stoker Award, the Locus Poll Award for Best Horror Novel, and the August Derleth Award for Best Novel. The rewards are many and rich for those who have the patience to allow Simmons to slowly unfold his epic tale. To do this, Simmons employs a large cast of characters, good and bad, that spans decades, from World War II through to the 80s, where he sets the bulk of his action. Be forewarned, anyone can die at any time and there is a lot of carnage spread out across its length. To boil the concept down to its barest foundation, *Carrion Comfort* deals with a small fraction of humanity that manifests a psychic ability, dubbed "The Ability," which enables them to overtake and control the actions of others against their will to commit heinous acts. However, though their bodies are no longer under their own control, these victims are perfectly aware of the horrifically shocking and murderous actions they are perpetrating. This creates a paralyzing terror deep within them that can then be fed upon by those with "The Ability," enabling them to remain young and vibrantly alive at their victim's expense. In this regard they are similar to vampires. We learn that those with this psychic gift play an escalating game among themselves in which they influence world events for their own perverse pleasure. However, over time they have left human debris in their wake, collateral victims who nurse a need for vengeance and justice that must be satisfied. These protagonists are deeply relatable, physically and emotionally damaged, and wonderfully fleshed out as they slowly find each other to form a strengthening group banded together in their pain and commitment to a life-or-death mission of destroying this evil cabal. Although it takes a while to get going, once it does this is a runaway freight train of brutal action and unbearable suspense that holds perhaps the single best ending to a novel that I have personally ever read with multiple plot threads smashing together in its final 100 pages. As great as anything written by Stephen King or Robert McCammon and leagues better than Dean Koontz, this is darkly grand entertainment of the highest magnitude and unreservedly earns my highest recommendation!

Steve Carroll

☠☠☠☠☠

THE CEREMONIES
T.E.D. Klein
1985 edition

"Themes and mythologies are reimagined and used to good effect..."

Jeremy Freirs is an overweight, struggling academic from New York who decides to spend a summer in the country to write his thesis, so far untitled, on the Gothic imagination. What Jeremy doesn't realise is that all of his actions and decisions are being manipulated by an ancient evil in the guise of an apparently kindly old man named Aloysius Rosebottom, aka Absolom Troett, in order to complete a series of rituals that will bring about the birth of a vast entity lying dormant within the earth. At one level this is an amusing social satire of a typically neurotic New Yorker finding it impossible to come to terms with the realities of country life, which is not the rural idyll he had imagined, and at another an entertaining dissertation on the history and themes of supernatural fiction. The Ceremonies is a long and leisurely book, but it is well worth a careful read, not only for the wonderful prose, but for the many hints, portents and details that Klein drops like a trail of crumbs to

---

BLOOD OF MY BLOOD Ray Feibush was a prolific cover artist for UK publisher New English Library, although rarely credited and his work sometimes confused with that of the superior Bruce Pennington, possibly due to editorial direction to ape Pennington's colourful and popular style.

THE CEREMONIES David O Connor art for the UK Pan edition from 1986 of Klein's only full-length novel.

CARRION COMFORT Stephen Brautigan cover for the 1990 Warner paperback of Dan Simmon's epic and award-winning novel.

show that nothing any of the characters do is the result of free will – the murderous Old One is always pulling the strings. The book is also a homage to Klein's favourite authors, in particular H.P. Lovecraft and Arthur Machen, and their themes and mythologies are reimagined and used to good effect, particular the sense of cosmic awe and universal evil that pervades the book. The one jarring note is the treatment of Mrs Poroth, the one person who knows exactly what is going on. At the start of the book, we are led to believe that she is a major character who will have a significant part to the play in the novel, but she appears less and less as the story moves along until she is summarily dispatched towards the end. Nevertheless, this a landmark book, a classic in the field.

James Doig

CHILDREN OF THE NIGHT
John Blackburn
1966

"Does a superb job of cataloguing the escalation in hatred radiated by the people infected by the children..."

Blackburn's fifth novel and regarded as amongst his best, it is a fast-paced account of a lost race whose confinement to a series of caves under the Cumbrian moors has mutated their physical and mental state. Riddled with worms that feast on their living flesh and capable of transmitting homicidal thoughts, the "children" emerge from their centuries of confinement to be greeted by a mixed crowd of do-gooders, the curious and the Army. It climaxes in an orgy of murderous fury shrouded in a cloud of gas (released by the story's heroes in an unsuccessful attempt to sedate the murderous children, but with shades of James Herbert's later *The Fog*) where Blackburn does a superb job of cataloguing the escalation in hatred radiated by the people infected by the children, with the internal dialogue between a high-ranking Army officer and his interfering wife an especially effective way of demonstrating this. A top-class example of Blackburn applying the approach of a straight thriller to bring realism and tension to an SF/horror conceit.

Justin Marriott

THE CONJURERS
David Gurney
1973

"Teases the reader as to what is real and what is parlour trick..."

Gurney excelled at using mundane settings for his occult horror, such as the quiet seaside town which hosts *The Conjurers*, where small-town gossips still speculate about the role mysterious clairvoyant Madame Jo played in the death of her errant husband. An opportunistic son-in-law blackmails Madame Jo into using her parlour to prey upon the gullible in search of answers and connections with dead loved ones, but soon finds he is dealing with dark forces beyond his or her control. Decorated with arcane symbols and quotes from Aleister Crowley, *The Conjurers* proudly displays its occult credentials, and the book carries a core of credibility. Gurney provides an inventive plot which teases the reader as to what is real and what is parlour trick - the conjuring of the title - but its over-emphasis on the mundane setting and dreary kitchen-sink drama tone makes it a slog through its meaty 284 pages, and Gurney certainly could have done with picking up the pace.

Justin Marriott

CHILDREN OF THE NIGHT Alan Lee's cover for the Panther 1970 paperback edition of Blackburn's superior horror-thriller shows the worm-riddled flesh of a lost race of underground dwellers now driven mad by the pain of being eaten alive.

THE CONJURERS Striking photo cover for the 1972 first paperback printing which capitalised on the public's salacious connection between sex and Satanism, which publishers were happy to perpetuate. There were two further paperback editions from New English Library.

CONTENTS FOR SALE Joel Iskowitz produced this archetypal haunted girl with creepy doll image for this part romance/part horror tale.

Panther Horror
Children of the Night
They crept out of the earth, gripping men in the terror of their ancient evil…
John Blackburn
Panther
586 02468 9

NEW ENGLISH LIBRARY
THE CONJURERS
DAVID GURNEY
'It is easy to call up demons, for they are always calling you…'
Aleister Crowley

CONTENTS FOR SALE
BECKY LEE WEYRICH
FIRST TIME IN PAPERBACK

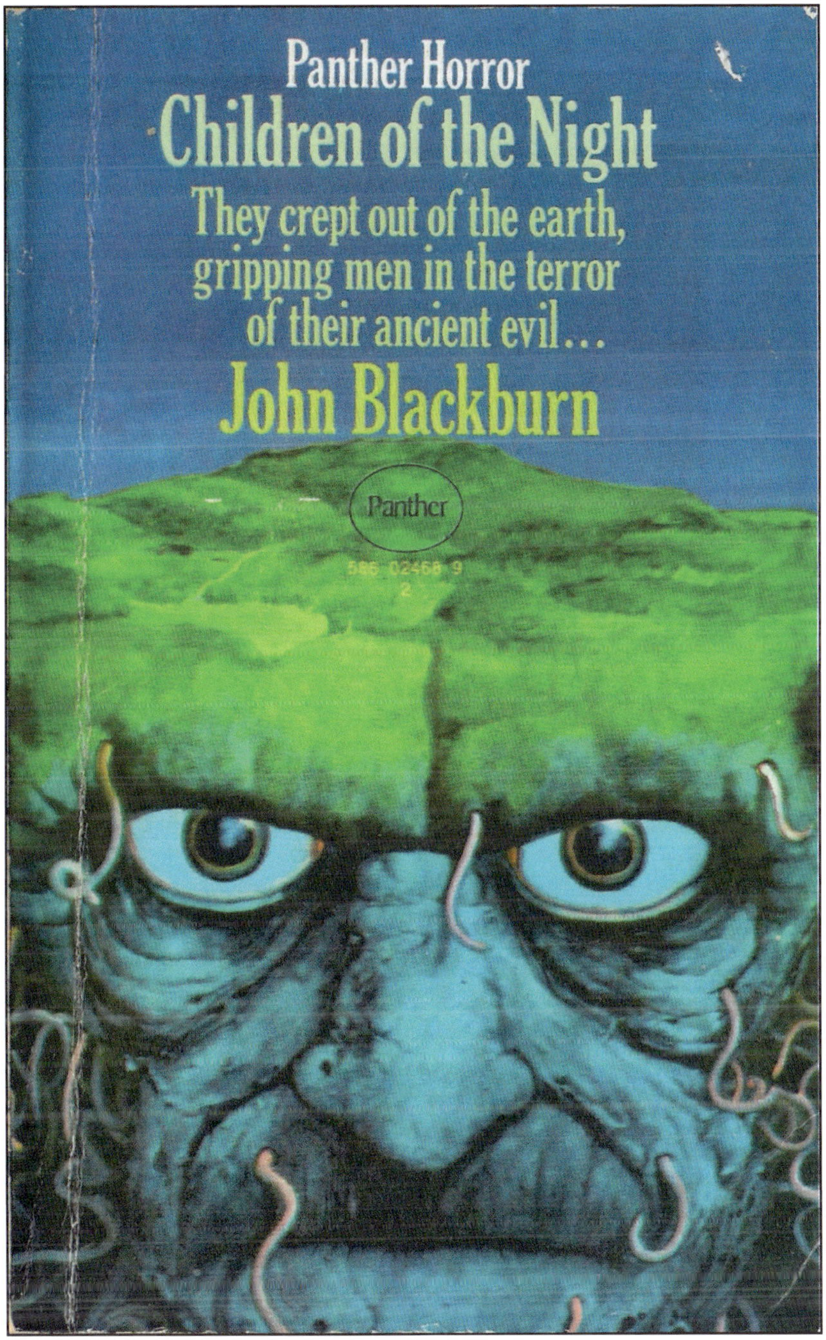

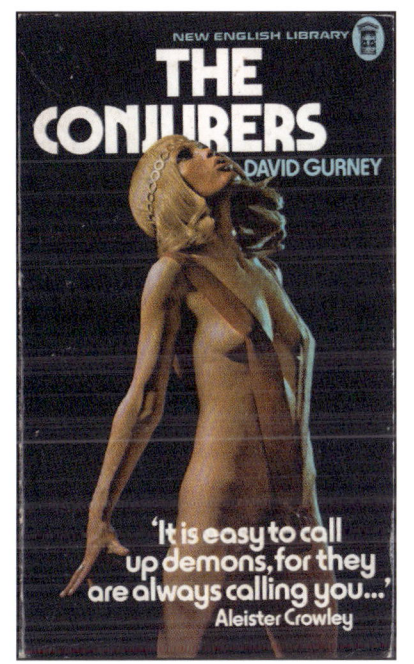

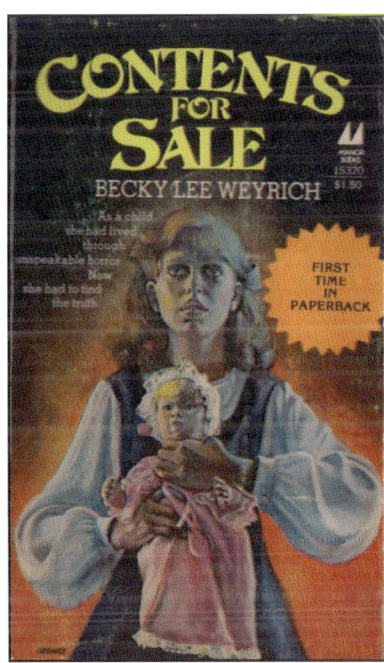

FANTASTIC FOCUS 1

PETER TREMAYNE

A MAINSTAY OF BRITISH HORROR IN ITS BOOM PERIOD OF THE 1970S WAS PETER TREMAYNE, ALTHOUGH HE WOULD NEVER ACHIEVE THE COMMERCIAL SUCCESS OF JAMES HERBERT OR THE CULT FOLLOWING OF GUY N SMITH.

Tremayne was the pseudonym used by Peter Berresford Ellis who, during the 1970s, was moving from trade journalism into authoring fiction, and would find his niche with the Sister Fidelma, historical detective series which are international bestsellers.

His horror fiction career began with the lightweight Hound of Frankenstein (1977) which was part of a short-lived foray into men's fiction by Mills and Boon, the famous specialists in romance. Tremayne also resurrected Dracula for a troligy of stories: Dracula Unborn (1977), The Revenge of Dracula (1978) and Dracula, My Love (1980). The latter is perhaps my favourite of his, with a strong romantic element and a sly sense of humour.

When not breathing fresh life into classic characters from literature, Tremayne would look to regional legends, such as the Cornish Morgow in *The Morgow Rises* (1982) derived from accounts of sea serpents off the ths shores of Cornwall, and at the other end of the country, *The Loch Ness Monster (1979)*. There was further sea-serpent thrills delivered by *Nicor!* (1987) as a dinosaur interferes with an oil rig in Central America.

Other mainstays of horror lore were used in Zombie! (1981) although in a more traditional manner on a Caribbean island, and Snowbeast! (1983), which in a less traditional manner gave the Highlands their very own Yeti. Angelus! (1985) is generally regarded as his best horror work, a showcase for the strengths that would transition him onto detective fiction, with an unknown murderer running rampant at an Irish boarding school.

The books often carried the most lurid art by the likes of Terry Oakes and Steve Crisp, which were very much at odds with the books gentle and quiet approach to creature-feature horror.

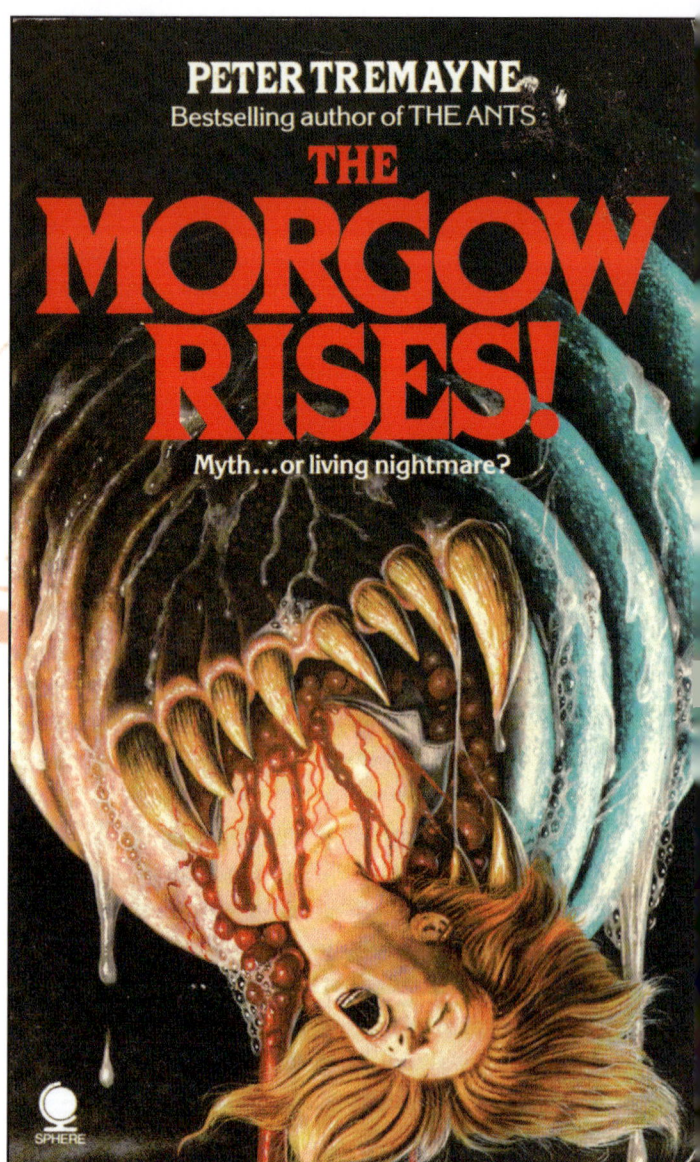

THE PSEUDONYM USED BY PETER BERESFORD ELLIS FOR A SERIES OF MILD YET ENTERTAINING HORROR NOVELS IN THE STYLE OF 60S HAMMER FILMS

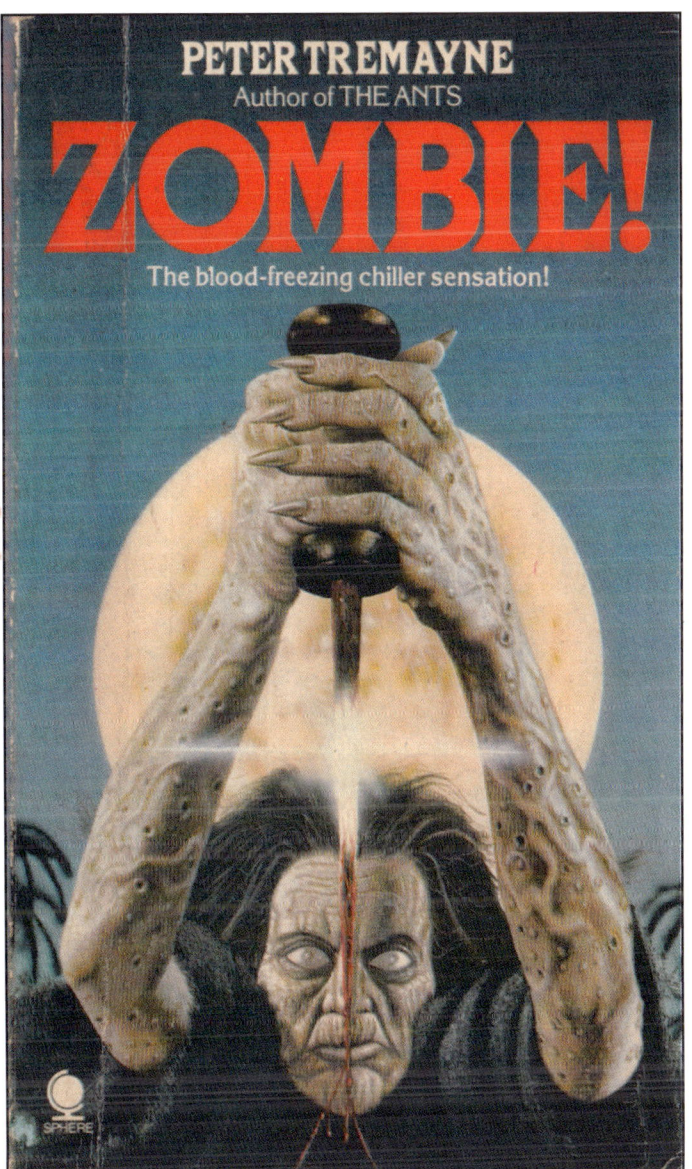

the paperback fantastic – HORROR

THE DEGENERATES
UK publishers New English Library with another of their trademark sex and Satanism photo-covers, although at least the contents of Shulman's potboiler throw in an orgy-loving cult, albeit at the insistence of her editors.

A CORBEN SPECIAL
Archetypal hyper-realised storytelling and visuals from Richard Corben, who always exaggerated the sex and violence in his material, even when adopting Edgar Allen Poe, whose Madeline is more pulchritudinous than previously suggested.

CONTENTS FOR SALE
Becky Lee Weyrich
1978

"Unexpectedly bleak ending lifts the book above the usual standard..."

Romance writer Becky Lee Weyrich's first novel. The back cover advertises the book as 'in the tradition of *The Omen* and *The Fury*,' but it is clear after reading it that this was a marketing ploy designed to cash in on the recently released and hugely popular films. The title and cover are unusually sedate for the period, and I got the impression that Weyrich was writing a romance novel before her publisher told her that supernatural horror was selling like hot cakes. The book is narrated by Kendra O'Neil, who works in an antiques shop and goes about buying stock at house sales and deceased estates. She hears that her childhood home is up for sale, the place where twenty years earlier her father had brutally murdered her mother before killing himself. Against the advice of her boss, she resolves to go back, ostensibly to buy the house contents for the shop, but primarily to find out what really happened that night. She ultimately uncovers the truth, but it is not nearly as startling as the back cover blurb suggests, and certainly not satanic or supernatural. Along the way she falls in love with and marries her childhood sweetheart, Link Fuller, who lost a leg in Vietnam, is harassed by the redneck chief of police, and must deal with recalcitrant family members trying to hide the truth. The book takes a surprisingly dark turn right at the end when Kendra is confronted by an awful apparition or hallucination: "The body inside the robe was slashed and bloody. One breast had been cut away entirely. A gash in her abdomen allowed her intestines to escape like writhing, slimy snakes. Below them, where pubic hair should have formed a dark triangle, glared bare bone devoid of hair or flesh." *Contents for Sale* is an entertaining and fast-paced read, and the unexpectedly bleak ending lifts the book above the usual standard of paperback originals of the time.
James Doig

A CORBEN SPECIAL
Richard Corben
Pacific Comics, 1984

"Fragile mental states and the pervading atmosphere of the decaying house..."

Artist Richard Corben had long been fascinated by the works of Edgar Allen Poe, adapting many of his stories into comic form with great aplomb at the Warren Magazines line of **Creepy** and **Eerie**. Pacific Comics granted him 28 full colour pages in a standard comic size to adapt the *Fall of the House of Usher*, and Corben seized the chance to deliver amongst his most innovative layouts (an element of storytelling he was not known for, as his work often resembled a series of panels of similar size to give the impression of being key frames cut from a film) and introducing a sexual element that Warren would not have permitted. There are only three characters in the story (four if you count the house, as Roger Corman would have done!), and Corben excels at communicating their fragile mental states and the pervading atmosphere of the decaying house. The final scene of a naked and voluptuous Madeline bursting through a door with bloodied hands in tatters from clawing out of her tomb is especially arresting. Although not quite as effective as Corben's masterful adaptation of Lovecraft's 'Rats in the Walls', which dealt with a similar theme of mental health issues passed through the generations like a family curse, which appeared in underground comic **Skull 5**.
Justin Marriott

THE DEGENERATES
Sandra Shulman
1970

"No doubting Shulman's efforts to deliver substance around the editorially stipulated volume of sexual shenanigans..."

Drifting through the glamour and glitter of Swinging London, a bitter and disillusioned David Sheldon is seduced by an evil cult whose members are taken from the rich, famous and powerful. Can he extricate himself from the satanic grip of the degenerates? Ambitious in the book's structure and thought-provoking ending, weaving in topical elements such as the Profumo scandal and the killing spree of the Manson family, there are no doubting Shulman's efforts to deliver substance around the editorially stipulated volume of sexual shenanigans. Unfortunately, stretched over 188 pages, the lack of sympathetic and relatable characters amongst the cast of high-society hedonists and Shulman's over-blown narrative style makes for a tortuous read. Legend has it that the editorial team at publishers New English Library insisted Shulman submit an orgy sequence for their approval prior to agreeing a book contract as they doubted she could deliver the racy goods.

Justin Marriott

THE DEMON
Written and Drawn by Jack Kirby

"Kirby's imagination is on overdrive, so it's a fun ride..."

Jack Kirby's time at DC Comics was filled with promise and disappointment. His initial offerings – the so-called Fourth World – didn't last long; certainly not long enough for fans of the individual titles (**Jimmy Olsen**, **The Forever People**, **The New Gods** and **Mister Miracle**), but they did introduced perennial baddie Darkseid to the DC pantheon (and led to Marvel creating their own version, Thanos). After these books, he tried again with **Kamandi**, **OMAC** and **The Demon**. The Demon in question is the servant of Merlin the Magician and enemy of Morgaine le Fey. With the fall of Camelot, Merlin puts himself into an enchanted sleep and he ties the Demon, Etregan, to a human, Jason Blood – who never ages. The comic then shifts to the modern day and age, and Blood is surrounded by several friends who alternately help him and get into trouble. When there's danger, Blood can switch into Etregan. And, of course, there's always danger! Kirby draws on mostly old horror films for his villains, including the Phantom of the Sewers (it's quieter there than in the Opera...); Baron Von Evilstein (and if you can't guess who that is without a hint – here's a hint: His assistant is Igor and he's creating monsters) and The Witch Boy, with a strangely human cat. There's even a one-armed policeman... Sure, it's derivative, but there's lots of Kirby's staggeringly brilliant artwork, and his imagination is on overdrive, so it's a fun ride.

John Peel

DEVIL DADDY
John Blackburn
1972

"Blackburn was evidently fascinated by religion..."

One of Blackburn's finest melding of the detective and horror genres. Marcus Levin, his spikey and fallible hero who is a survivor of a concentration camp and now a knighted bacteriologist, uncovers a bid to destroy the world by a religious cult. Blackburn's characters typically seek out scientific responses to supernatural phenomena, with the user of a super-computer central to Levin's mission. In this way, Blackburn's stories are remotely related to A E Van Vogt, the SF iconoclast whose early SF pulp work typically used science rather than ray-guns to solve life-threatening problems. Blackburn was evidently fascinated by religion and uses a biblical character as the focal point for the book's revelation, leading the reader through a set of plot progressions until it becomes the most natural answer to the mystery Levin is faced with. The book's opening set-piece lingers in the mind; an interview with a seemingly immortal recluse who lives in a totally sterile environment and wears long gloves to avoid touching anything or anyone. He has curated a secluded gallery room, in which hangs a series of paintings in the style of world-masters, but so depraved in their subject matter and so expensive to accumulate, they are assumed to be brilliant forgeries.

Justin Marriott

DEVIL DADDY Ian Miller produced a nightmarish image of melting flesh and religious iconography for Blackburn's excellent horror thriller with a biblical twist.

SAGA OF THE SWAMP THING The Demon made a striking and brilliantly executed appearance in the Alan Moore scripted run of DC's muck monster. Illustration by John Totleben and Stephen Bissette from issue 27 in 1984

THE THING THAT SCREAMS "Jolly" Jack Kirby does horror in this panel from the July 1973 issue of **The Demon** which pays homage to the unmasking sequence in the film *Phantom of the Opera*.

The Paperback Fanatic – Horror

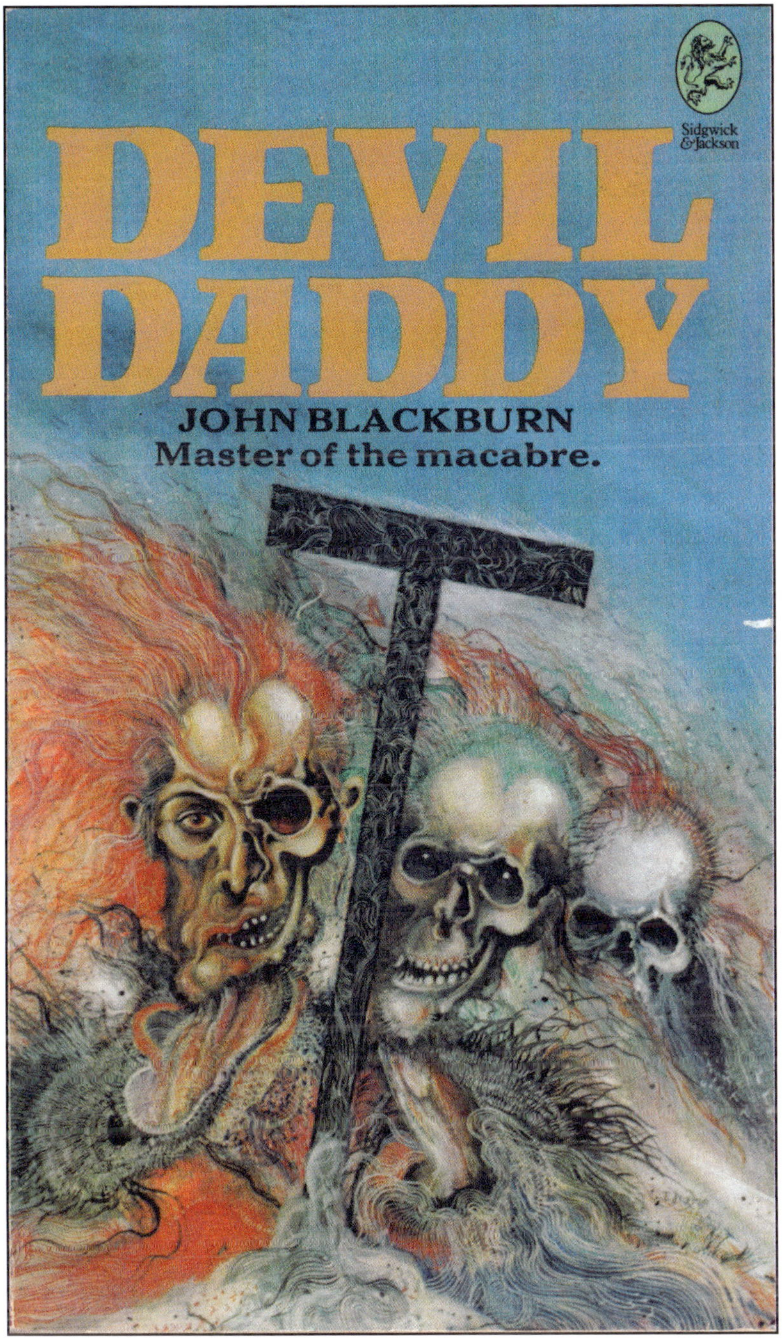

DELL
2102
1.95
In a quiet New England town man has lost control, and the beasts are loose.
The Dogs
ROBERT CALDER
A novel of pure, snarling terror "far better than JAWS!"
—THE KIRKUS REVIEWS

Simon Raven
Doctors Wear Scarlet
Patrick MacNee stars in DOCTORS WEAR SCARLET with Peter Cushing as Dr Goodrich
Panther

. . . is obviously destined to be the most smashing popular success since Sapper —Spectator
3/6
Doctors Wear Scarlet
SIMON RAVEN

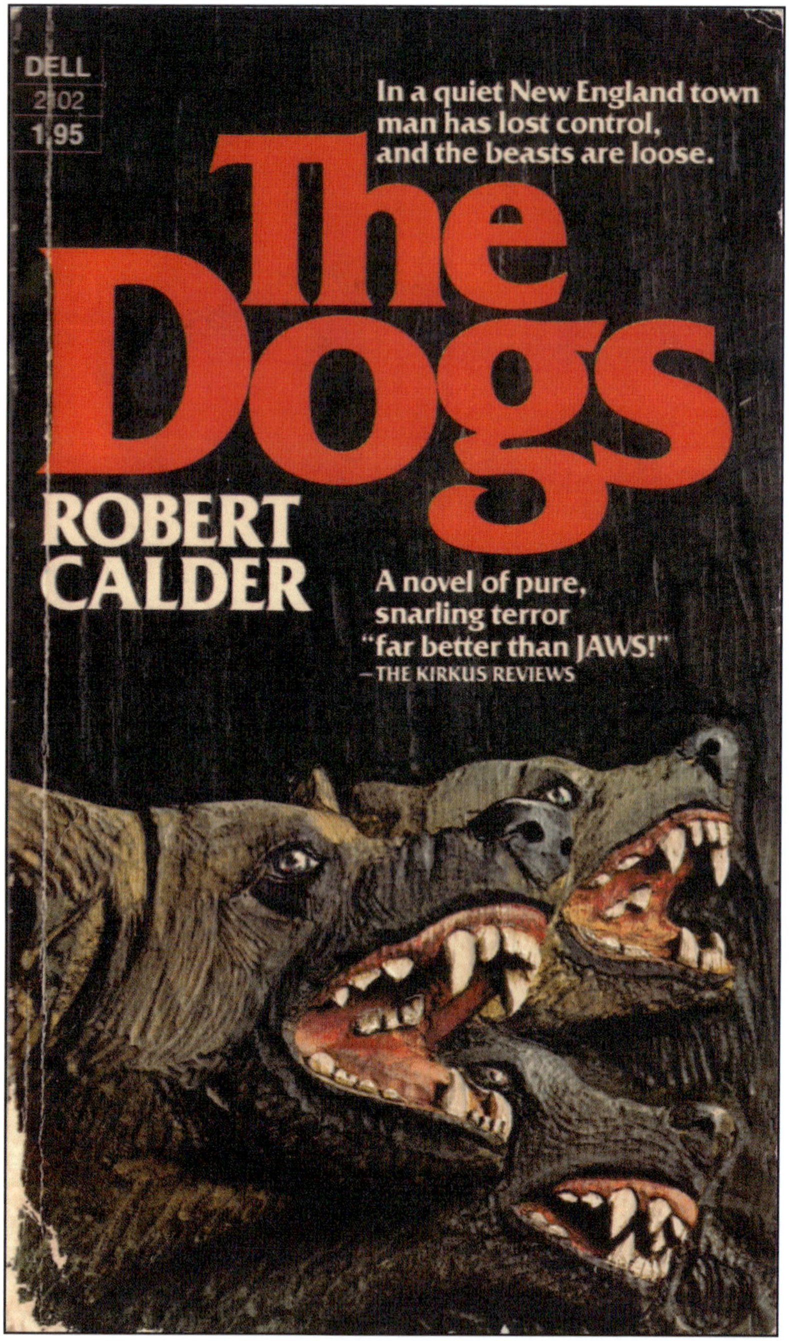

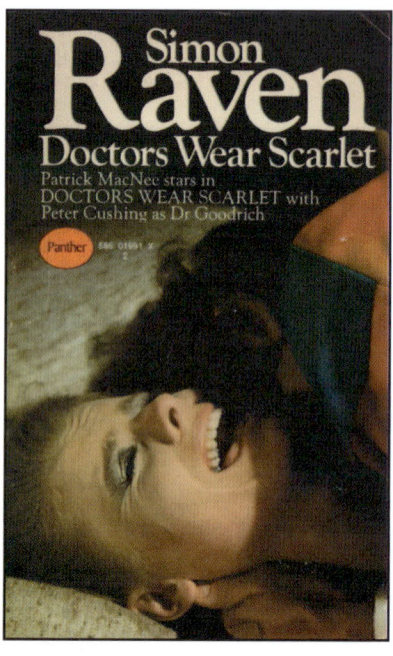

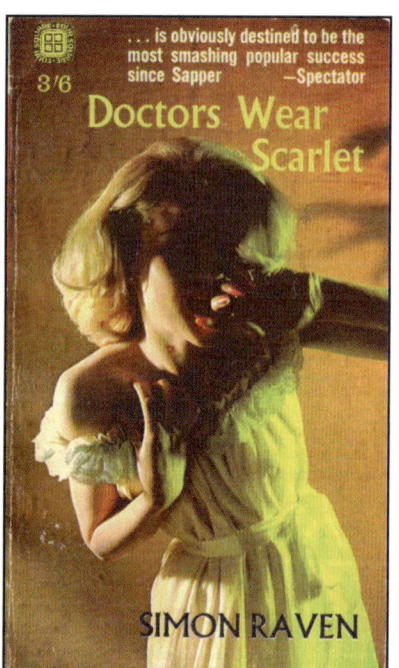

DOCTORS WEAR SCARLET
Simon Raven
1960

"An original and unusual take on the vampire theme…"

Karl Edward Wagner included this novel in his **Twilight Zone Magazine** list of 13 'Best Supernatural Horror Novels', though it isn't a supernatural novel at all. It's an original and unusual take on the vampire theme, which Raven uses to good effect to show the moral decline and ultimate tragedy of an intelligent and thoughtful young man whose freedom is taken away by people who think they have his best interests at heart and who want to control him. The book is narrated by Anthony Seymour, whose school friend Richard Fountain has gone missing in Greece. Seymour is questioned by John Tyrrel of the Metropolitan police and relates at length Fountain's life at Charterhouse school, Cambridge University and the army, focusing on a few anecdotes that present Fountain as resourceful and socially popular but with a violent streak. At Cambridge, Fountain studies classics with a particular research interest in ancient Greek rites and religion. He is taken under the wing of Walter Goodrich, a Cambridge don who plans for him to marry his daughter Penelope and obtain a fellowship at his college. Fountain tries to assert his independence by forming a close friendship with a young, hedonistic undergraduate, Piers Clarence, which annoys Goodrich and worries Penelope, who is in love with Fountain. To separate the two, Goodrich arranges for Fountain to undertake research in Greece for a year or two. While in Greece he disappears amid rumours he is involved with a mysterious Greek woman and has committed some unnamed but dreadful crimes. Seymour, Clarence and Roddy Longbow, Fountain's superior officer when he served in the army, travel to Greece to find Fountain and return him to England. As they travel around Crete and the Greek islands, they learn that Fountain had fallen in with a Greek woman named Chriseis, who Piers realises is a vampire, though not a supernatural being: *'she's a woman all right, and she's a mortal woman. But she is the inheritress, if I am not mistaken, of an old and particularly obscene tradition.'* Enlisting help from the local Greek population they manage to rescue Fountain, but not before Roddy is killed. Piers dispatches Chriseis by strangling her and banging a stake into her heart with a rock. Weak and still under the influence of Chriseis, Fountain returns to Cambridge, but Goodrich resumes his efforts to control him and map out his future. At a college feast in his honour (from whence the book's title is derived), Fountain decries Goodrich in an erratic speech after which he collapses. Penelope takes him off to his rooms, and soon afterwards Fountain is found drinking the blood of her dead corpse. Fountain takes an overdose of a tranquiliser given to him by Piers and is found dead the following morning. Certainly worth reading, though the potentially fascinating character of Chiseis is wasted and she hardly appears in the novel – Raven is more interested in the blokes and their psychology and motivations.

James Doig

THE DOGS 1977 paperback edition from Dell with an effective wood carving cover which communicates the elemental nature of the dogs.

DOCTORS WEAR SCARLET Panther UK issued at least three editions of Raven's novel, with this 1969 being a movie tie-in, presumably not helped by the actual film calling itself *The Bloodsuckers* when released.

DOCTORS WEAR SCARLET Although Panther would become the UK publisher who led with paperback editions of Raven's difficult to classify work, the first paperback edition to appear in the UK was this 1962 Four Square.

THE DOGS
Robert Calder (Jerrold Mundis)
1976

"Rendered in presumably accurate but devastating detail…"

Alex Bauer is a university lecturer trying to escape his past who adopts a stray puppy, whom he monikers Orphan, unaware it has escaped from a military experimental facility where it has been conditioned as a highly dangerous attack dog. The books plots switches between Orphan, who deserts the lecturer and fulfils his violent destiny, and Bauer who heals through the love of an idealistic student. In the same way as *Jaws* wasn't just about a giant shark, *The Dogs* has depths, and you can tell Calder truly cares about all his characters in a way that I very much admire, applying as much care to his depiction of Orphan as the humans. Truly the most horrific sequence in the book focused on a dog-fighting ring which is rendered in presumably accurate but devastating detail. Calder was a pen name for Jerry Mundis, who also wrote as Eric Corder (mainly historical fiction focused on the slave trade), Julia Withers (gothics), Franklin W Dixon (shared house pseudonym for the **Hardy Boys**), and Jack Lancer (teen fiction). With a strong personal interest in dogs, Mundis bred his own German Shepherds and trained attack dogs.

Justin Marriott

DRACO THE DRAGON MAN
Cyril Donson
1974

"So inept that even the legendary Badger Books may have hesitated to publish..."

Written in a breathless tabloidesque style using block capitals and endless ellipses, in a failed shortcut to inject some spice and vigour to this ludicrous tale, this is a book so inept that even the legendary Badger Books may have hesitated to publish. World-renowned archaeologist Damon Draycott discovers a race of mind-reading lizard-men living in the bowels of the earth. Struck by a curse, Draycott becomes a fire-breathing, flesh-devouring and sex-crazed were-dragon! Donson had contributed to a number of short-story magazines in the 1960s, specifically the many crime anthologies that proliferated at that time, so possibly Donson's talents were particularly unsuited to the horror genre. After a series of hardback westerns in the 1980s, Donson's trail goes cold – maybe he returned to his dragon people in the bowels of the earth?

Justin Marriott

THE DREAMERS
Roger Manvell
1964

"Compelling plot and creepy moments..."

I hadn't heard of this novel before and was pleased to pick it up at a local second-hand bookshop for $3.50. This is the Corgi paperback published in 1964, which is quite scarce, but the US Bantam edition published a year earlier is more common and can be picked up cheaply online. It was first published in 1958 by Gollancz when the author Richard Manvell was Director of the British Film Academy (he was the inaugural Director from 1947 to 1959). It's quite possible he wrote the book with a film in mind, and in fact Ray Bradbury wrote a script for it but the film was never produced. It's a short, fast-paced novel with a nice premise – set in a small English village in the Thames Valley, a woman Jane Fettes is badly shaken one night by a terrible nightmare. She tells the dream to a friend, Myra Calloway, who has the same nightmare that night. When Myra's hen-pecked husband, Albert, is debilitated by the same nightmare, Jane calls in the village doctor, Stanley Morgan. Dr Morgan believes the recurrence of the nightmare can be explained psychologically and he advises the three people not to tell anyone else about the dream and to try to forget it. Nevertheless, he relates the dream to his love interest, the beautiful village divorcee, Joanna Martin. That night Dr Morgan has the nightmare and is lucky to survive it, but when he visits Joanna, he finds her dead in her bed with a look of horror on her face. Dr Morgan rings his journalist friend, Andrew Desoutter, who he had met in Africa when they were both working there. On inspecting Joanna's body and hearing the story of the recurring nightmare, Desoutter brings in his friend, Dr Amenu King, an African negro and an expert on dreams. From the moment Dr King is introduced, the theme of racism is paramount to the book, though Manvell's exploration of it comes across as crude and simplistic to a contemporary readership. Dr Morgan is revealed as a rabid racist due to his experiences in Africa. However, the brilliant and compassionate Dr King is able to bring him around through his handling of the case. Firstly, he realises Joanna isn't dead, just comatose, and then he realises the nightmare results from a dream-curse that was meant for Dr Morgan because of his failure to save a woman in Africa. In a scene reminiscent of the *The Exorcist*, Dr King manages to exorcise the dream-curse from Joanna and kill the African sorcerer in a battle of wills. Cured of his racism, Dr Morgan returns to Africa to work after marrying Joanna. *The Dreamers* has a compelling plot and creepy moments – certainly worth seeking out.

James Doig

DRACO THE DRAGON MAN
Cyril Donson was one of those hugely prolific writers who kept magazines and papers well provided for. His better work was short stories for **The London Mystery Magazine** in the late 60s.

THE DREAMERS
Josh Kirby produced many horror and SF covers for UK publisher Corgi which were typically great. His version of a gothic romance with its heroine fleeing includes a truly nightmarish apparition to chase her from the house.

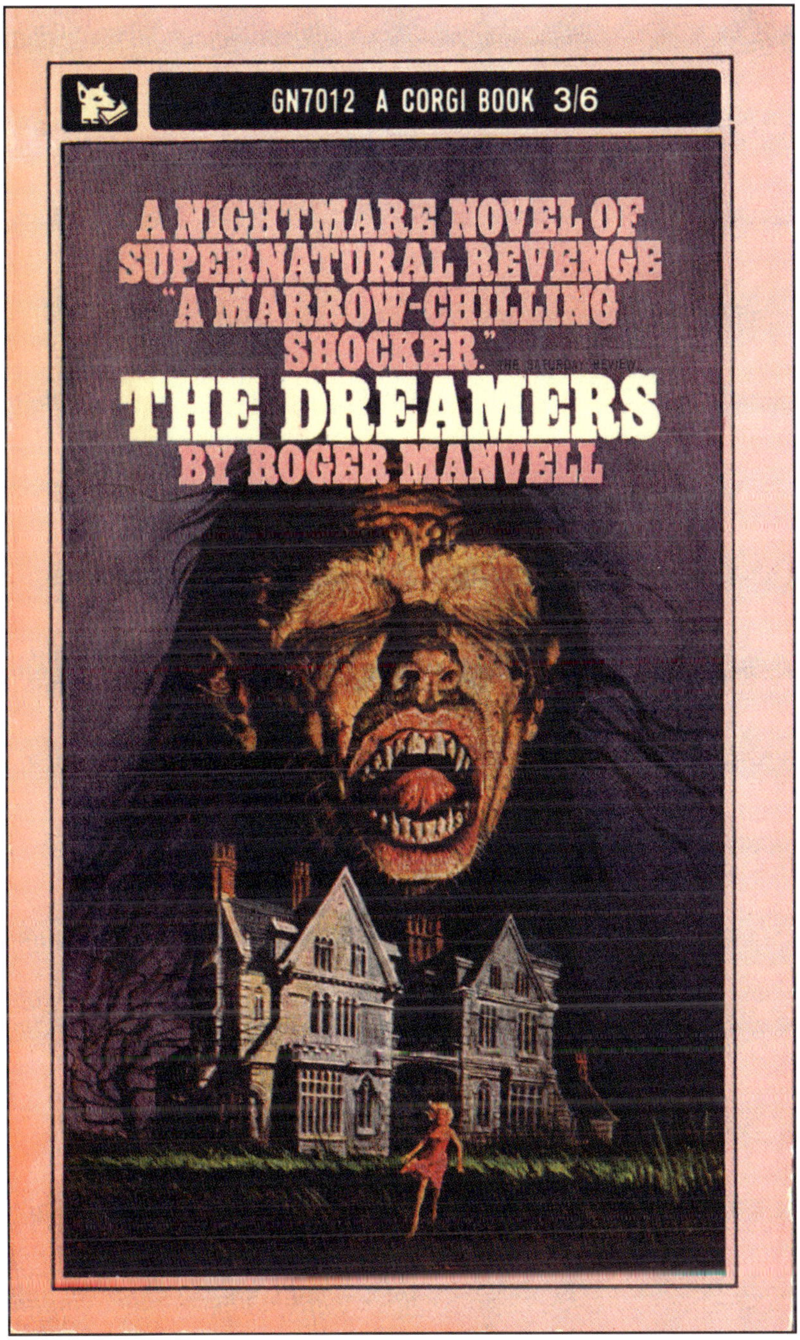

FANTASTIC FOCUS 2

SIGNET ON THE RAMPAGE

THE 'ANIMALS ATTACK' AND ASSOCIATED 'NASTY' GENRES WERE VERY BRITISH ONES, WITH THE SUCCESS OF JAMES HERBERT AND GUY N SMITH DRIVING MANY COPYCATS. IN AMERICA, THE BESTSELLING STEPHEN KING WATERED DOWN THIS TREND TO EXPLICIT AND SHORT-FORM FICTION. SIGNET WAS THE LEADING PUBLISHER IN THE US THAT TAPPED INTO THE POPULARITY OF THE BRITISH BOOKS.

Killer Flies (1983) did what it said on the cover. Kendall's name didn't appear on any other books, so likely a pseudonym.

The Scourge (1980) was part of a series of solidly entertaining horror novels written by Scott Gronmark under the pseudonym of Sharman.

Panther! (1981) featured not one, but twenty, black panthers on the loose in the New York streets following a publicity stunt for a film gone wrong.

Killer Crabs (1979) was the best of Smith's series, set in Queensland with a crew of undesirables in search of the proceeds of a bank job, fighting one another and the giant crabs.

The Survivor (1977) was a reprint of one of Herbert's more disappointing reads, albeit still carrying a great sting-in-the-tail.

Fangs (1980) sets a venomous snake on the loose in a luxury apartment block. William Dobson was the pseudonym for Michael Butterowrth.

Lair (1979) was Herbert's sequel to *The Rats* and amongst his best in a strong catalogue, probably the best of the sex and violence loaded 'when animals attack' books.

The Cats (1979) was Sharman's written-to-order cash-in on *The Rats*.

Hounds of Dracula (1977) was a tie-in to the obscure film perhaps best remembered for its experimental electronic soundtrack. This book originated at a short-lived UK publishers Everest which was managed by Ken Follett a future bestseller.

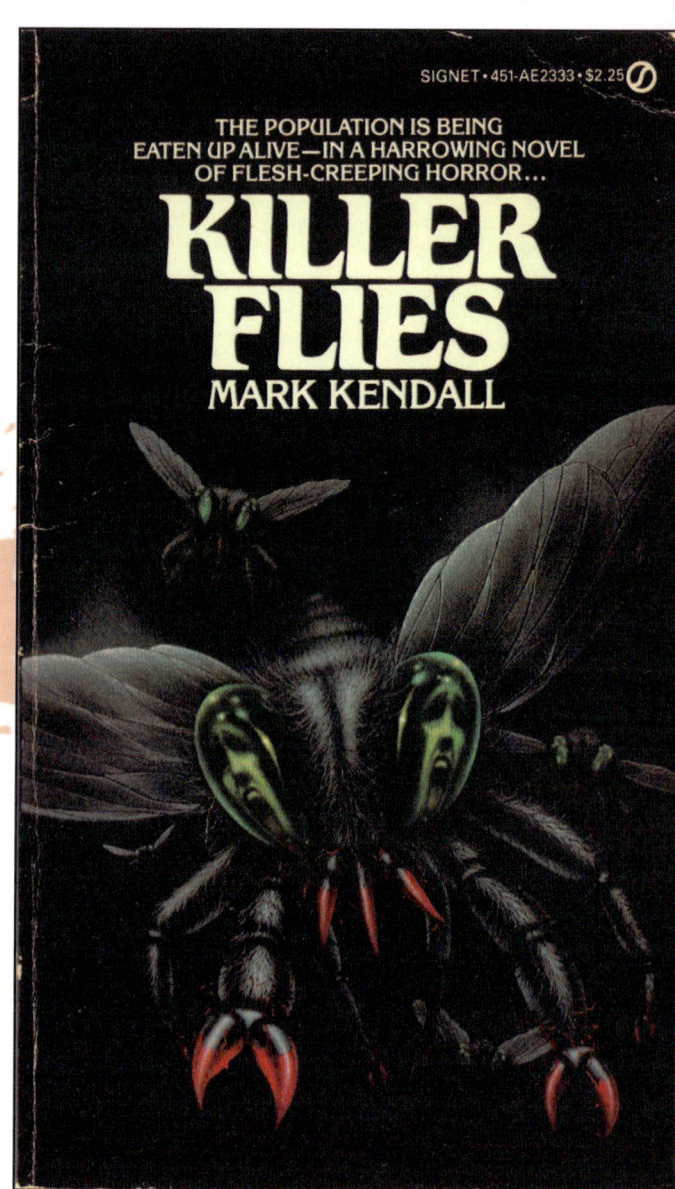

US PUBLISHER SIGNET BOOKS PRODUCED A STREADY MIX OF BRITISH REPRINTS AND US ORIGINALS WITH UNIFORMLY ATTRACTIVE COVERS

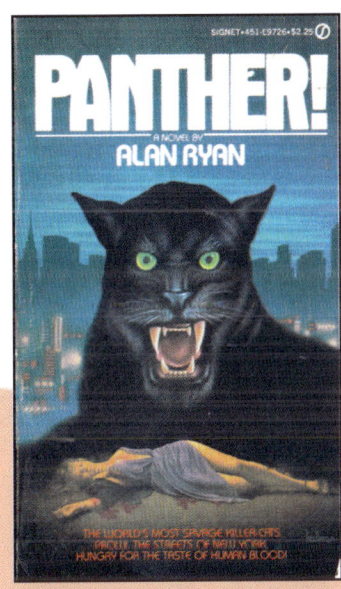

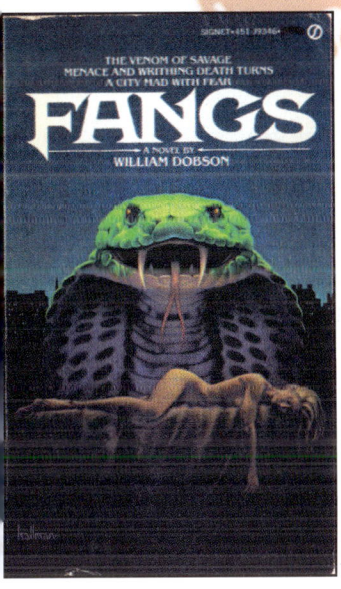
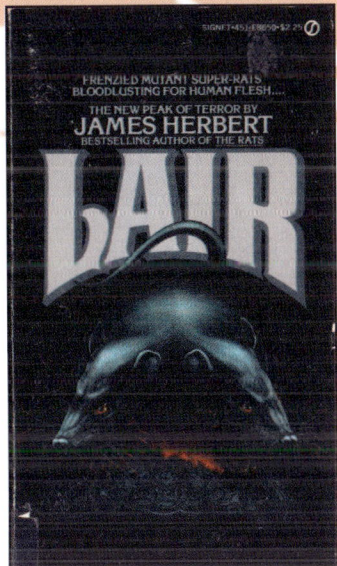
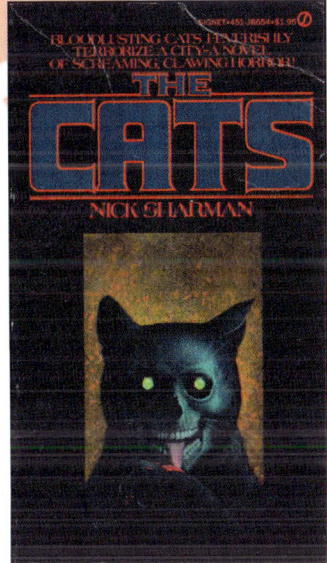
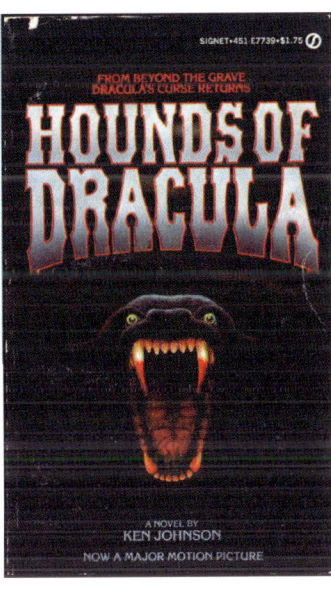

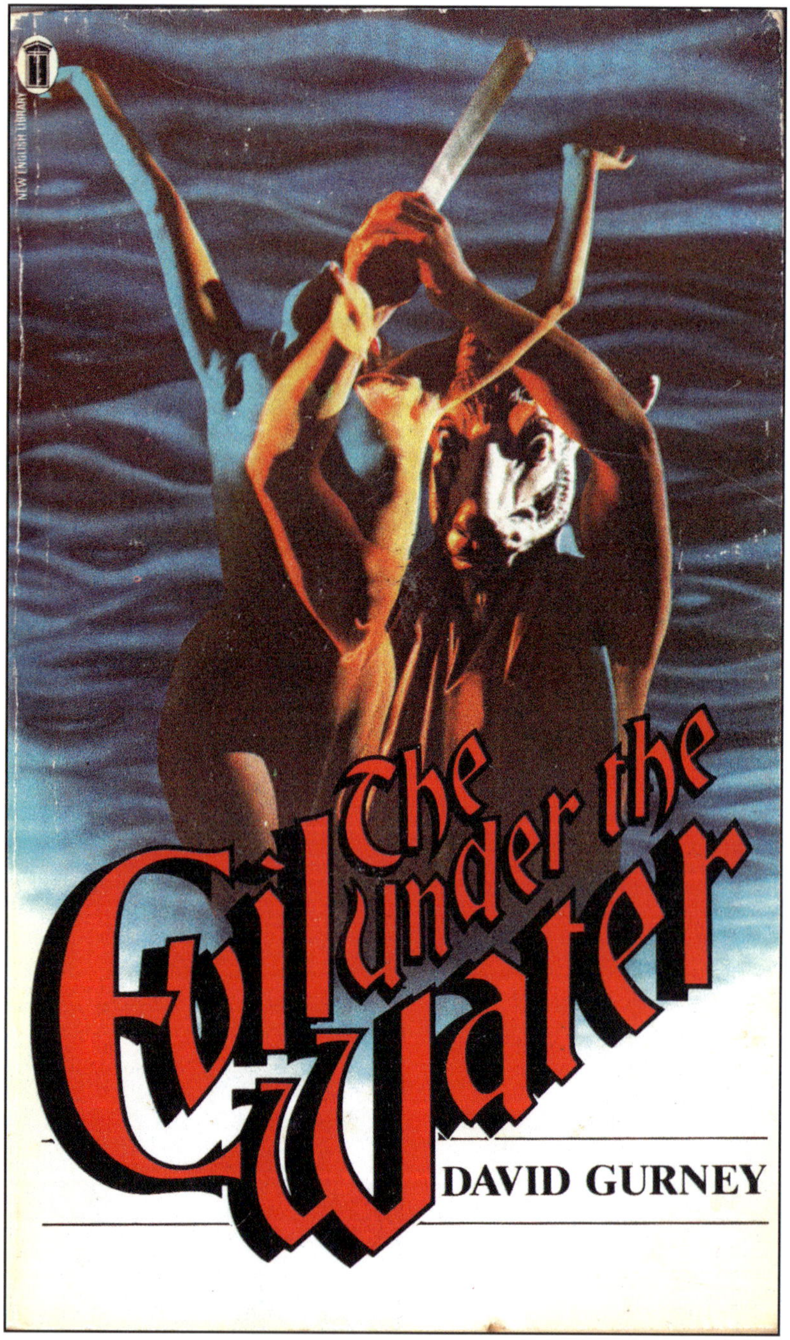

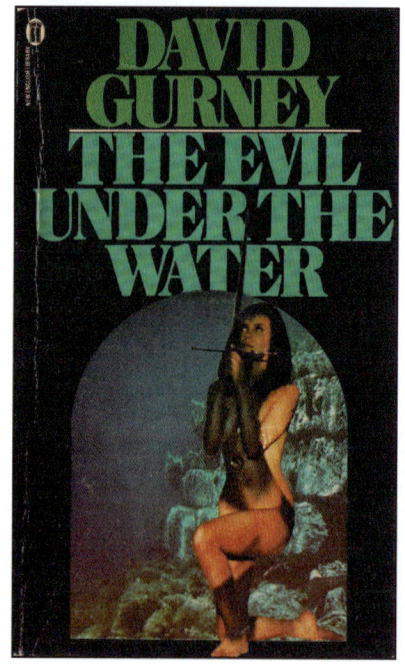

THE EVIL UNDER THE WATER
David Gurney
1977

"At times threatens to collapse under the weight of its own ideas..."

This effective occult-thriller opens with a signature David Gurney plot device of a disappearance (see also *The Conjurers* and *The Devil in the Atlas*), and this time it's virginal Julie Jordan who goes missing following a mysterious party she attended. All of the signs point towards a satanic ritual having taken place at the party, and when her boyfriend Mike Benson is also kidnapped and the investigating officer put under a curse, it's down to Inspector Farmer of the Occult Investigation Branch of the CID to save their lives. Yes, that bastion of British policing apparently has an Occult Investigation team! Part Ed McBain procedural, part Dennis Wheatley hair-em scare-em, with SF elements for good measure, *The Evil Under the Water* is crafted with great care but at times threatens to collapse under the weight of its own ideas. It will test the patience of the reader anticipating schlocky dressings of horny occultists cavorting in the buff and horny goat-demons materialising. Not that Gurney is averse to delivering skin-crawling set-pieces, as evidenced by the fate of the officer whose effigy is placed in tank of giant ants; witnessing the man plagued by the sensation of insects crawling over his skin, an observer notes that the plugs preventing the ants entering his bodily orifices haven't been removed- yet! If this book had been published half a decade earlier, I'm sure publisher New English Library could have turned the exploits of the Occult Investigation Branch into a longer-running series.

Justin Marriott

THE 16TH FONTANA BOOK OF GREAT HORROR STORIES John Holmes provided a typically disquieting image for this well-regarded series. Holmes is probably best remembered for his connected images for H P Lovecraft editions from Ballantine in the US.

THE EVIL UNDER THE WATER Two paperback editions from New English Library which both appeared in 1977. Peter Haining who was editor at NEL had stated that Gurney's real name was Patrick Dair, although on-line sources suggest it was David Groom.

THE 16TH. FONTANA BOOK OF GREAT HORROR STORIES
1983
Edited by Mary Danby

"Toothless and lacking in a cutting edge..."

This collection from the long-running rival to the more famous **Pan Book of Horror Stories** is a mix of the newly commissioned with budget-conscious reprints, wrapped up with the Fontana trademark of the editor providing the final story. Representing all genres of horror and with a line-up of competent authors, this anthology still left me unmoved and unshaken, and as I shut the pages the stories disappeared from my mind like cobwebs dusted away by a diligent cleaner. Flicking through it now, the stories which did leave at least some impression are, 'The Farmer' by Steve Rasnic Tem, where the punchline is obvious to everyone bar the young man who will be responsible for ensuring a healthy crop, 'Mother's Day' in which the punchline would have been totally shocking were it not quoted on the book's back cover, 'Switching Off' which was an EC-esque tale of revenge upon a bullying teacher, and a Ramsey Campbellesque story 'Blackberries' by Roger Clarke, which made little sense but delivered a cloying atmosphere and a nauseating apparition. In reflection, perhaps the books were edited with a young adult market in mind, hence them seeming toothless and lacking in a cutting edge when read in 2022.

Justin Marriott

FRANKENSTEIN'S TREAD
Jean-Claude Carrière

"All you could want in a black and white B-movie starring Frankenstein's monster..."

In the late 50's at the height of the first wave of "monster-mania" Mary Shelley's enduring creation Frankenstein got to go on six more rampages, in France of all places! Academy Award winner Jean-Claude Carrière is mostly known as a screenwriter but also was a novelist and sometimes even an actor. Plus, he also wrote about Gouroull, his own personal name for Frankenstein's monster, who's a bit like the novel and a bit like the movies. A hulking beast of an undead man with glowing yellow eyes, grey skin, and a thoroughly evil

disposition. The books weren't translated into English for many years, depriving us of a wonderful interpretation of one of the icons of horror. They were also written as straight pulp novels for the 'Fleuve Noir' line as Benoit Becker and Carrière/Becker fully deliver on the heavy pulp. What we got here is a moody, wild, dangerous and dirty ride on an island that has all you could want in a black and white B-movie starring Frankenstein. It's really one of my favourite interpretations of 'ol Frankie. There are gruesome murders on fog-dense landscapes, a mad scientist building a woman, voodoo zombie's, the ripping of throats with teeth, scared fisherman, terrified widows being pursued by undead men. It's a wonderfully gothic potboiler, chock-full of mood and atmosphere and manages to not skimp on the horror and action. It doesn't reinvent the monster-wheel, it just takes it on a perfectly told spin around the block.
Roy Nugen

GHOST RIDER
Marvel Comics
Writers and artists vary

"Marvel really didn't know quite what to do with him..."

He began his career as a Western hero, but as the TV Westerns died out, Marvel jumped onto a different bandwagon, and he was completely reborn as a daredevil biker. Johnny Blaze worked the circuit with his best friend, Crash Simpson and his gorgeous daughter, Roxy. But Crash was doomed to die, and Johnny strikes a bargain with the Devil to try and save his life. Not a smart idea, of course, since the Devil always cheats. Johnny is possessed by a demon and becomes the Ghost Rider – complete with a blazing skull and the ability to shoot off hell-flames. He has one chance to save his soul – through the innocence of Roxy. But the Devil knows this and targets her for destruction. Lots of supernatural shenanigans follow, as Johnny becomes a Hollywood stunt rider, and then goes off to try and discover himself. Is he human any longer? Will he ever be free of the Ghost Rider? The plotline tends to vary as writers shift about. Sometimes he's even fighting supervillains – and he even became a member of the superhero group "The Champions" for that magazine's short run. Marvel really didn't know quite what to do with him, and he tended to suffer as a result. But he was popular enough to get his own movie, and he turns up from time to time to this day.
John Peel

HEADHUNTER
Michael Slade
1984

"Retains its ability to shock and engage..."

An impressive and ground-breaking example of the cross-over between horror and police procedural begat by the likes of *Silence of the Lambs*. And whilst the four-author team behind the Michael Slade pseudonym aren't quite in Thomas Harris' league (the ending to *Headhunter* still confuses me, despite multiple re-readings), this is a much more transgressive and challenging read than any Harris bestseller, demanding much of the reader with its detail, time zone and perspective switching, as well as its truly morbid atmosphere. There are aspects of the human condition portrayed in this book which are as shocking now as they were then, and Slade collectively picks apart the legend of the Canadian Mountie by re-examining a slice of brutal history. Plenty of twists and turns, uncompromising storytelling that verges on the documentary, a flawed hero and a welcome heroine, *Headhunter* has stood the test of time and retains its ability to shock and engage.
Justin Marriott

GHOST RIDER Left is a detail from Mike Ploog's 2013 recreation of his work for the first cover of **Ghost Rider** from Marvel Comics in 1972. Ploog was a master of the comic book medium but was tempted away to work in film design on projects such as John Carpenter's *The Thing* and *The Dark Crystal*.

FANTASTIC FOCUS 3

FRANKENSTEIN

FRANKENSTEIN WAS BEGUN IN JUNE 1816 WHEN MARY WOLLSTONECRAFT GODWIN (LATER SHELLEY) WAS 18, COMPLETED IN MAY 1817 AND PUBLISHED IN JANUARY 1818. HOW WAS IT THAT A TEENAGER COULD CONCEIVE OF AND WRITE SUCH A FASCINATING GOTHIC HORROR/SCIENCE FICTION NOVEL?

Born in August 1797, Mary Godwin had quite a convoluted life. Mary ran away with the older Percy Shelley when she was 16, fleeing from England to Switzerland since Percy was abandoning his pregnant teenage wife of 3 years and their 13-month-old daughter. Disowned by both families, Mary had to suffer the pregnancy, birth and death of her first daughter Clara while she was 17, give birth to son William in January 1816, and juggle a 6-month-old baby while moving around Europe to evade Percy's creditors. All the moving around led to a published travelogue and also provided details of Lake Geneva and its surroundings for *Frankenstein*. Percy drowned in 1822. Mary supported herself and surviving son Percy Florence by writing numerous novels, short stories, biographies and travelogues until her death in 1851. Including, *Frankenstein*!

Frankenstein is a young man at college who cobbles together a variety of body parts and uses electricity to bring his creation to life, then immediately flees. Left alone with no resources, his creation finds food, saves a small child from drowning, learns to speak and read, and then returns to ask Franknestein make him a companion. When Frankenstein reneges on his promise, his creation vows vengeance.

Frankenstein was written over 200 years ago, which shows in the dense sentence structure and is also very different from the film versions. The book shows Frankenstein's inability to ever acknowledge how wrong he was to create life and then abandon it. Although you can get it for free on-line since it's out of copyright, I highly recommend the Berni Wrightson edition since the illustrations are tremendous. Seeing many of those illustrations in person when they were loaned to the Minneapolis Institute of Art by Guillermo del Toro just underscored how wonderful they are. Few horror novels have stood the test of time like Frankenstein. If you haven't read it yet, you should wait for a dark and stormy night and crack it open! *Penny Tesarek*

THE STORY OF MARY SHELLEY IS EVEN MORE TRAGIC THAN HER MOST FAMOUS CREATION, THE MONSTER STITCHED TOGETHER BY FRANKENSTEIN

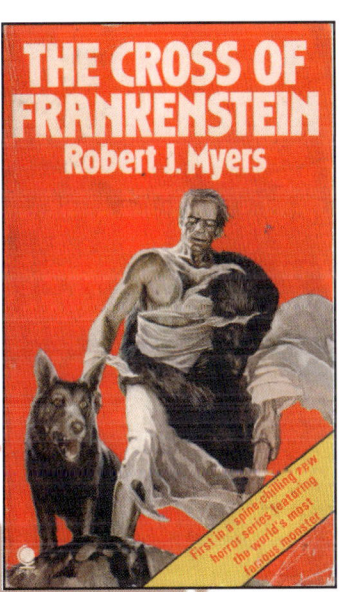

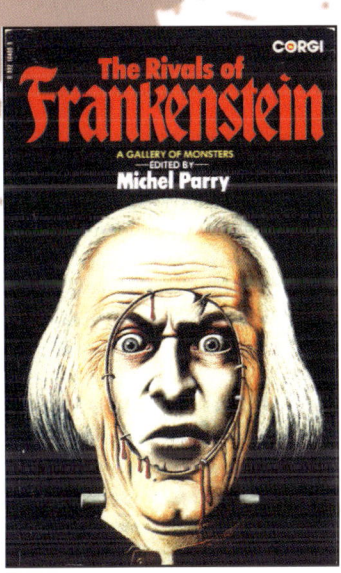
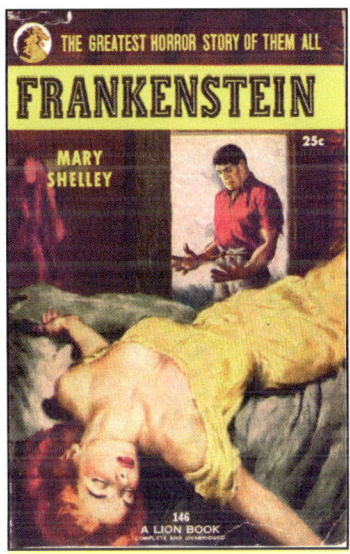

HOMUNCULUS
Kenneth Rayner Johnson
1982

"Might give the impression that this book is some uber-sleazy and outrageously bad-taste classic..."

I know nothing about the author of this grubby (in places) and padded-out (in ALL places) story of a demon-kid who kidnaps an inventor's daughter to impregnate her with baby homunculi. But based on the quotes from various occult books Johnson includes at the beginning of each chapter, the interminable rituals the villains recite over multiple pages, plus his authorship of two non-fiction titles, I guess he was another of those real-life occultists who took their studies seriously and reluctantly turned their hand to pulp-fiction to pay the bills. See also Gerald Suster and Jack Shackelford. I was able to skip page upon page of incantations without losing the narrative thread which is bereft of tension and surprise. There are several passages - which if quoted in isolation might give the impression that this book is some uber-sleazy and outrageously bad-taste classic in the style of *Eat Them Alive* – but they are few and far between. The cover is some sort of classic, but if accurate to the book's description, would feature a third head.
Justin Marriott

THE HORROR IN THE HEIGHTS
Sir Arthur Conan Doyle
1913

"Something for everyone!"

Horror stories by the creator of Sherlock Holmes? Yes, indeed – like any number of his contemporaries, Doyle was a prolific author of short stories, and this collects 14 of his spooky stories. They're a product of his age (early 20th Century), so they're very mild by modern-day standards, but he was always a superb craftsman, so his imagination runs unfettered. The title story, for example, relies on the "new" invention of aviation, and the fact that nobody really knew then what might lurk in the rare atmosphere. His speculation of predatory life way above the clouds is intriguing. Then there's a delightful mummy story ('Lot No. 249'), a brilliant parody of a ghost story ('Selecting A Ghost') in which a snobby newly wealthy boor tries to buy himself a family ghost, and the very creepy 'The Parasite', concerned with hypnosis by someone with no limits of morality. There's even a monster-on-the-rampage tale set it the Blue John mine in Derbyshire. Something for everyone! As I say, they're low-key for people more used to slasher movies, but they're delightfully written and just plain good fun.
John Peel

THE HORROR STORIES OF ROBERT E. HOWARD
Robert E Howard
2008

"There isn't a bad story in the lot ..."

Best known as the creator of Conan and credited more broadly as the founder of the sword and sorcery genre, Robert E. Howard dabbled in just about every other genre during the pulp years. From westerns to sports stories—and everything in between—as diverse as his subject matter was from tale to tale, one would think his success would vary as greatly. But, in this reader's opinion, his fiction never failed to hit its mark. Case in point: his foray into the horror genre. A master wordsmith, Howard had a talent for penning evocative prose. Time and again, his colourful descriptions of setting and characters effectively painted word pictures. This talent transferred well to his horror tales, and Del Rey did an excellent job in collecting all of them into one volume. Packed with over 500 pages of Howard goodness, this tome pulls text directly from Howard's own manuscripts (some **Weird Tales** editors were known for heavy-handed—and often unnecessary—revisions), including fiction, poetry, and unfinished fragments. As in other Del Rey Howard editions, this title is lavishly illustrated with many painted and pen and ink pieces (Greg Staples being the artist this go-round). Here, you'll find tales of voodoo, werewolves, sea monsters, mummies, supernatural revenge, haunted objects, and horrors returned from the grave. Standout stories for me include "The Horror from the Mound," "Pigeons from Hell," and "The Shadow of the Beast"—but make no mistake, there isn't a bad story in the lot. So, whether you're a fan of Robert E. Howard or of pulp horror in general, if this book isn't already in your collection, do yourself a favour and rectify that soon!
S Clayton Rhodes

THE HOMUNCULUS

The name Ken Rayner Johnson only appeared on four paperbacks, all being in the horror genre. Two were movie tie-Ins, *Hounds of Dracula* (1977) and *Blue Sunshine* (1978), the third was *The Succubus* (1979) which was an occult thriller, and the final was this disappointing effort. The uncredited cover artist did their best to "sell the sizzle".

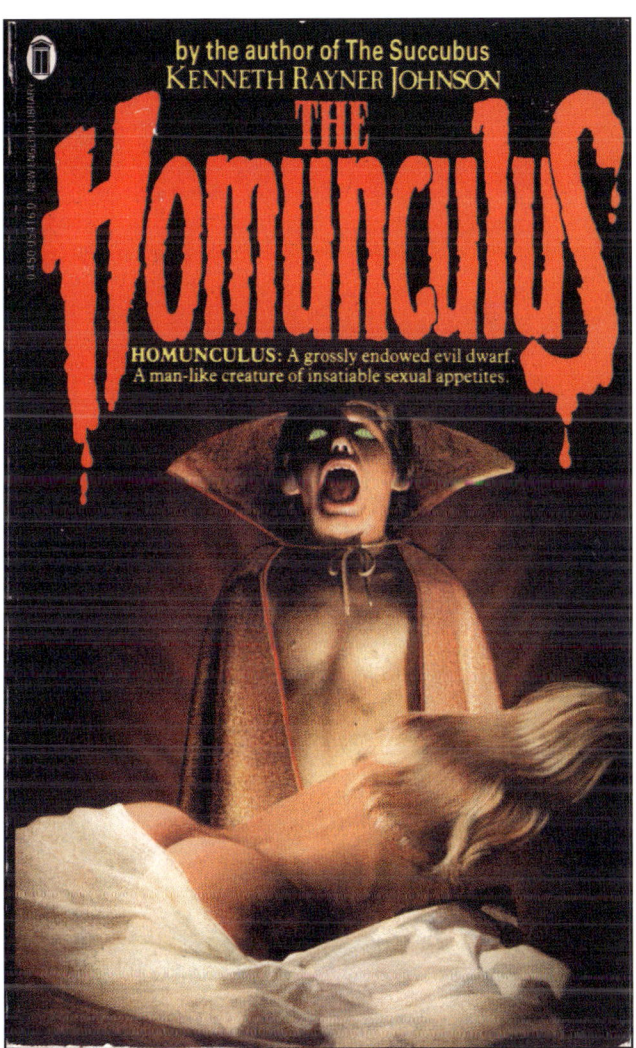

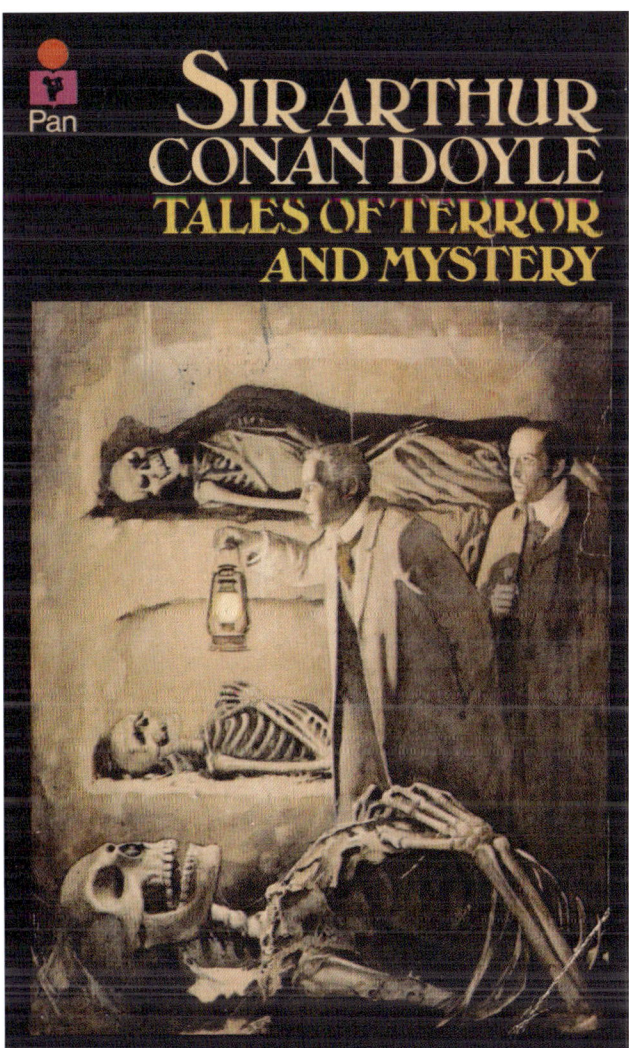

THE HORROR OF THE HEIGHTS opened this 13-strong selection of Conan Doyle's short fiction. It was published in the UK by Pan in 1978, with a watercolour painting by Alan Lee on its cover. His distinctive style was best suited to fantasy and he is best known for the heavily illustrated *Faeries* (1978).

THE PAPERBACK FANTASTIC - HORROR

THE HOUSE ON THE BORDERLAND
Hodgson's classic text has been blessed by a number of excellent covers over the decades. Ian Miller's illustration for this Panther UK 1972 edition is the finest in my eyes, with its multiple levels capturing the suggestions of inter-dimensional gateways and other worlds.

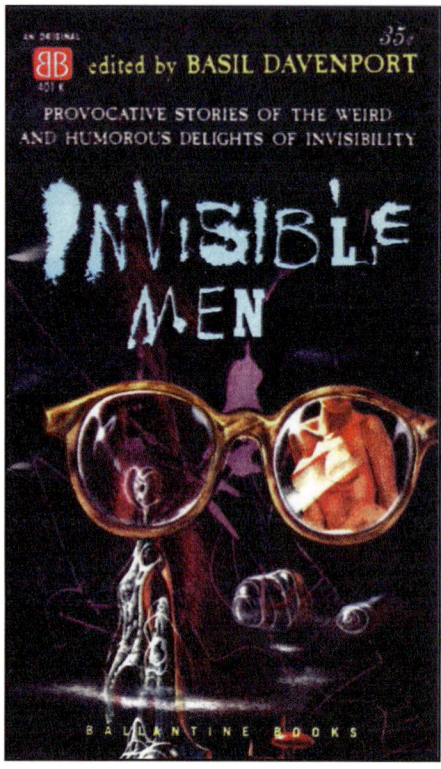

INVISIBLE MEN
Another typically brilliant and surreal cover for Ballantine from Richard Powers. When revisited after reading the anthology, it becomes clear as to how Powers captures key elements of the stories.

HOUSE ON THE BORDERLAND
William Hope Hodgson
1908

"If you haven't had the pleasure of reading this well-crafted piece from the past, I suggest correcting that immediately..."

Another oft overlooked gem of the past is an early entry in the "cosmic horror" category, predating even H. P. Lovecraft's efforts in this arena. *House on the Borderland* concerns itself with the discovery of a manuscript—as so often is the premise of stories of this nature do. The journal alludes to events experienced by a seeming eccentric who inhabited an unusual mansion where the readers now stand. The author gives an account of being accosted by horrific hybrid half-human half-swine creatures in the shadowy fringes near and around his home. It's ambiguous as to whether the writer is a victim of madness or if the events described actually occurred, but it is suggested the house was an epicentre where parallel existences collided. So much is packed in this little chestnut, but I won't spoil things by giving away further details. In a word, *House on the Borderland* is simply "masterful." Lovecraft himself described the tale as a dark work "of the first water." In fact, as mentioned previously, this yarn covers similar ground as Lovecraft's work. Only Hodgson did it first, and I would daresay his writing style is more accessible than Lovecraft's—gasp, yes, I really did just say that! If you haven't had the pleasure of reading this well-crafted piece from the past, I suggest correcting that immediately. Night Shade Books has produced a handsome set of Hodgson's collected work, so you won't have far to look in securing a copy.

S. Clayton Rhodes
☠☠☠

INVISIBLE MEN
Edited by Basil Davenport
1960

"Lives up to the promise of being provocative and humorous..."

The final in a trio of uneven anthologies Davenport edited for Ballantine, and the only anthology I am aware of that is dedicated to invisible men. I get the impression that Davenport was scratching around for horror material, with a number of stories which didn't quite match the title. It certainly lives up to the promise of being provocative and humorous, although lecherous could be added to that description, with 'Love in the Dark' by H L Gold living up to its title and especially 'The Weissenbroch Spectacles' by L Sprague De Camp and Fletcher Pratt being an 8-page joke about X-ray specs and large breasts. And it was only recently – honest – that I noticed the reflection on the glass lens on Richard Power's painted cover. There were two outstanding stories, with 'Shuttle Bop' by Theodore Sturgeon stretching the theme but making up for it by being 3 stories in 1. From whimsical fable to graphic horror to revenge themed twister, it's as if H P Lovecraft wrote for EC Comics. Henry Slesar's 'The Invisible Man Murder Case' was also a marginal qualifier for theme, but a romp of a pointed portrayal of an author in the Mickey Spillane mould, hugely successful yet craving the critical acclaim which is absent. The extracts from his books and the resultant reviews are huge fun. The pickings were thin, and little wonder there have been no subsequent editor's brave enough to use the theme of invisibility.

Justin Marriott
☠☠

THE ISLAND OF DR. MOREAU
Joseph Silva (Ron Goulart)
1977

"Struggled with a very bad script, but he didn't struggle very hard..."

Okay, I admit it – I bought this tie-in to the 1977 Burt Lancaster film because it had pretty pictures on the cover (Barbara Carrera!), and I assumed it would be a reprint of H.G. Wells' original novel. It wasn't – it's a novelization of the film script based on Wells' book. My next thought was: "Who the heck would have the sheer nerve to (basically) rewrite Wells?" The answer turned out to be Ron Goulart, under his Joseph Silva pen-name. I can only assume he did it because the film's producers wanted the book to be as far removed from Wells' original as their movie was. For those of you unfamiliar with the original (scary) story, Dr. Moreau is insanely determined to turn animals into men through incredibly painful surgeries and drugs. He succeeds to a degree, but they are constantly slipping back into their animal states, and he punishes them in the House of Pain. Goulart struggled with a very bad script, but he didn't struggle very hard. It's H.G. Wells lite – very lite.

Like a diet soda, it looks a bit like the original, but with all the body, taste and interest removed. Only try it if you're like me and collect tie-in editions. Or because you like pictures of Barbara Carrera.
John Peel

KILLER CRABS
Guy N Smith
1978

"A greater sense of humour than the snobby detractors of his books had given him credit for..."

Smith's books are as British as fish and chips, set in the locales and country-side that he loved, so I suspect that the action in *Killer Crabs* was relocated from wind-swept Wales of its predecessor *Night of the Crabs*, to the tropical setting of Queensland in order to appeal to a worldwide market (when picked up by New American Library in 1979, it was the first of Smith's books to be reprinted in the US). *Night of the Crabs* was only ever intended as a one-off, but its surprise success dictated there would be a sequel, and why not go for it in terms of a wider market. It definitely is bigger and bolder than the rest of the series, as the pages of *Killer Crabs* swim in bodily fluids spurting from cast of losers and low-lives ripped from a hardboiled crime novel, who bed and betray one another in the search of the proceeds of a bank-job, which happen to be stashed in the giant crab's spawning grounds. Climaxing in a fiery inferno in the mangrove swamp, *Killer Crabs* is priceless, with Smith doing a sterling job of intertwining the disparate characters and plots, whilst still finding time to throw in a few unexpected twists and plenty of crab attack scenes dripping in bad taste and camp excess. *Killer Crabs* also offers evidence that Smith had a greater sense of humour than the snobby detractors of his books that sprang up in the late eighties had given him credit for. In one scene, a survivor of an attack on his boat by the crabs blindly jumps into the sea in the pitch black of night. Floundering in the darkness he grabs a flotation device that turns out to be a severed leg. If that's not enough to draw a chuckle, Smith then has the unfortunate crab-bait recognise from the leg's training shoe that it's his!
Justin Marriott

MANSTOPPER
Douglas Borton
1988

"Characterization of the dogs is as raw, flesh-hungry killing machines..."

A later entry to the killer canine genre and was certainly the rawest and grittiest of the demented dog titles I've read. A punk on a thrill-kill spree unknowingly frees four highly trained attack dogs, and led by their alpha Razor, the furry foursome go on the rampage until their trainer and a local sheriff team up to track and destroy them. Unlike the other books in this category, Borton's characterization of the dogs is as raw, flesh-hungry killing machines, with little of the hand-wringing, preaching more typically encountered where the author must make clear that it's man who is the monster. Razor is a Doberman Terminator, with the final sequences where he relentlessly pursues his foes through an old-fashioned funhouse complete with a Hall of Mirrors and revolving tunnels, worthy of anyone's reading time.
Justin Marriott

MAYNARD'S HOUSE
Herman Raucher
1980

"Despite the lack of much happening, we find ourselves unable to stop reading..."

Maynard's House presents an intriguing premise: shortly following service in Vietnam, Austin Fletcher inherits a small cabin in wooded upstate Maine from his recently killed in battle comrade, Maynard Whittier. We come to learn the area may be under the influence of a sort of residual witchcraft, and what

---

KILLER CRABS An iconic cover for another of Guy N Smith's guilty pleasures. The font design for the title is especially distinctive and the colour choice reflects the glowing yellow of the crustacean's eyes.

THE ISLAND OF DR MOREAU The top right edition is the movie tie-in published by Ace Books and the bottom right is the Science Fiction Book Club hardback edition. Both in 1977.

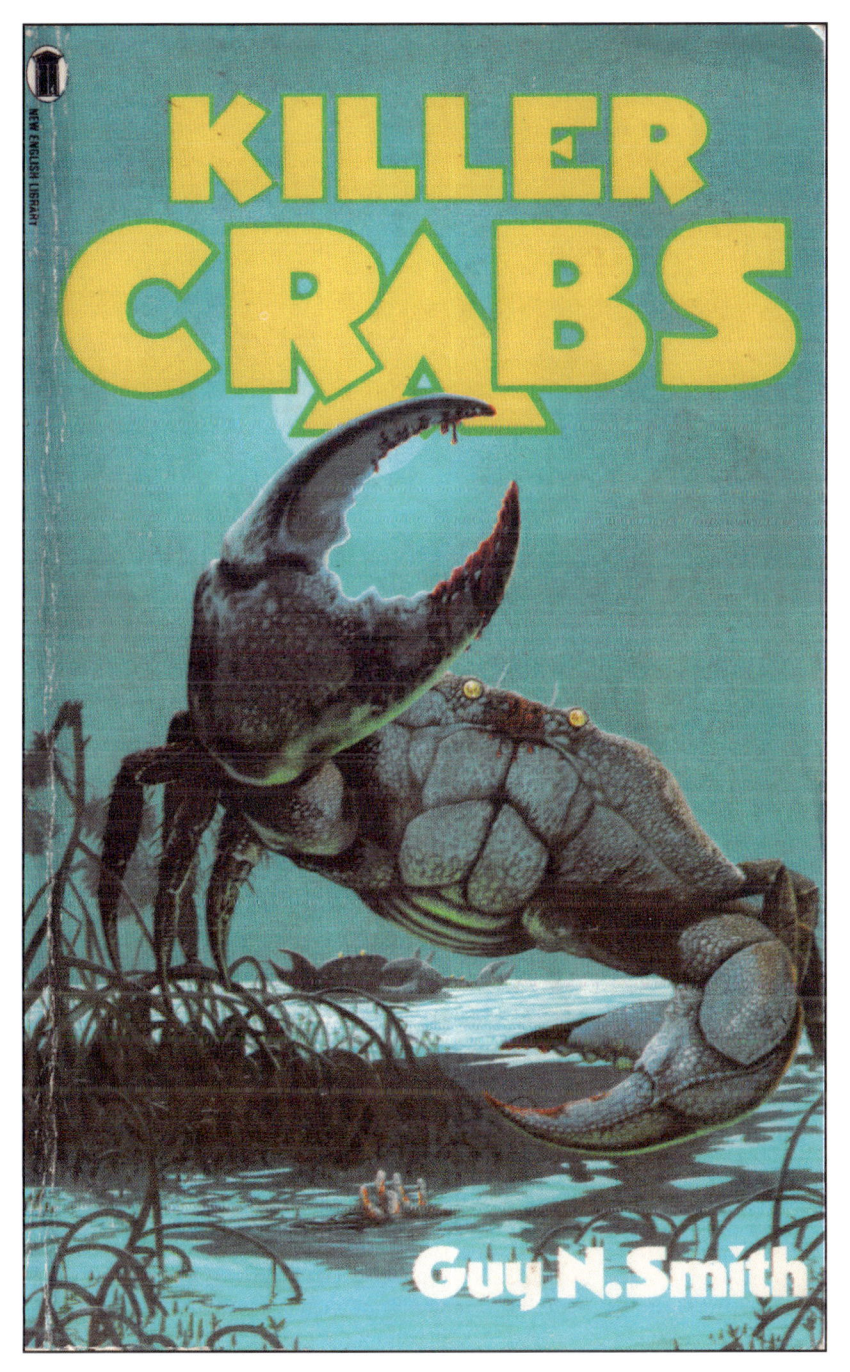

KILLER CRABS — Guy N. Smith

THE ISLAND OF DR. MOREAU — original novel by H.G. Wells, screenplay adaptation by Joseph Silva

The Paperback Fantastic – Horror

FANTASTIC FOCUS 4: CHARLES BIRKIN

THE KISS OF DEATH
Charles Birkin
1964
"Sardonic, snobbish and spiteful..."

Championed by the best-selling occult author Dennis Wheatley, Charles Birkin's written output of short stories were gathered into 7 collections from 1964-70, showcasing a mastery of the 'conte cruel' which earned a controversial yet enduring reputation within the horror genre. Although at surface level Birkin's stories follow the standard twist formula, they typically carry no supernatural elements and often end in unbearable cruelty to the young and the innocent. There is no reassuring punishment of evil or the depraved in Birkin's world. No subject is off limits to Birkin, with this collection taking in cannibalism, child murder, sex-crimes and the Holocaust. It kicks off with the titular short in which leprosy is intentionally transmitted by a spurned lover and moves onto the nauseating The Kennel in which a vengeful husband imprisons his unfaithful and now pregnant wife, sustaining her with a thick broth of a mysterious meat. The horrors of WW2 are central to 'The Hitch' and 'The Mouse Hole', with the latter a masterful exercise in tension, as a mother must make a choice between her son being cooked alive in the oven in which he is hiding from the SS or betraying the French Resistance. 'Some New Pleasures Prove' is the most conventional horror story in this gruelling collection, with an isolated lady menaced by an escaped sex-criminal who Birkin depicts with a frightening reality decades before the serial killer story was to be in vogue. Sardonic, snobbish and spiteful, these stories are the best in their field, but will not appeal to all.

Justin Marriott

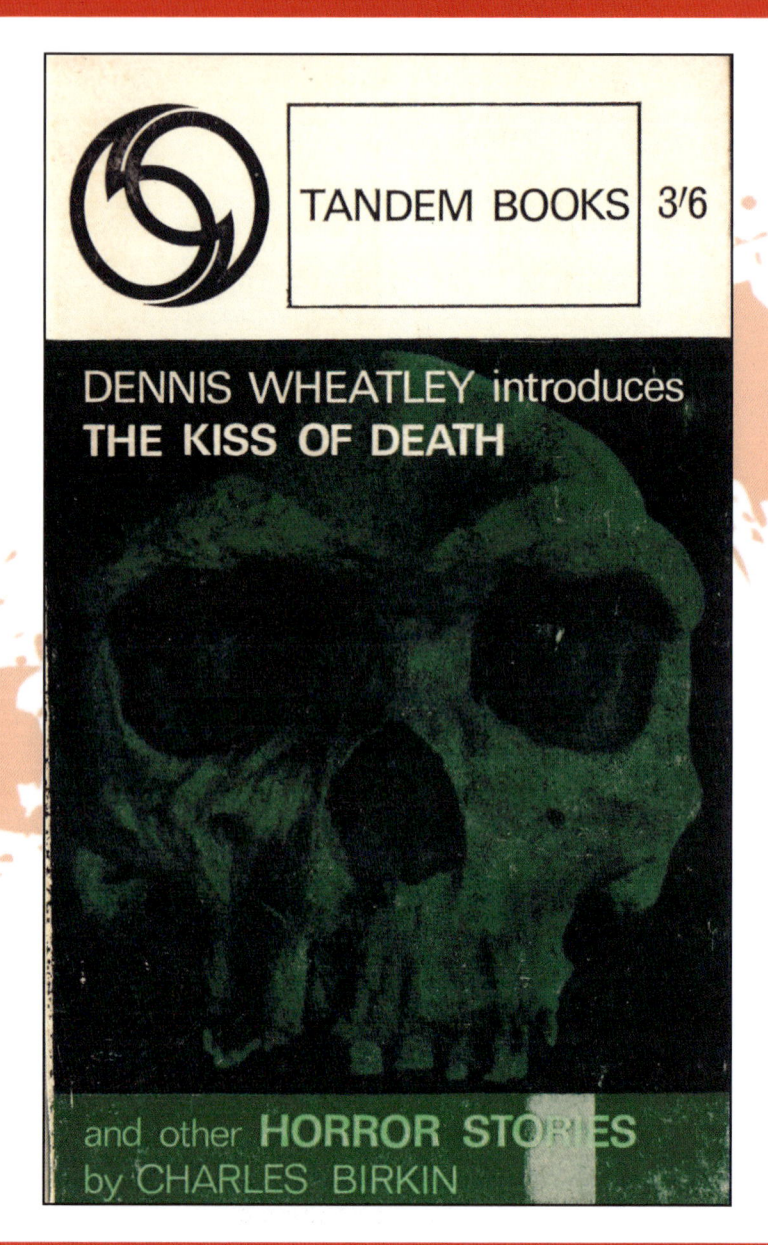

CHAMPIONED BY DENNIS WHEATLEY THE PIONEER OF OCCULT FICTION, CHARLES BIRKIN WAS THE CONTROVERSIAL MASTER OF THE CONTE CRUEL

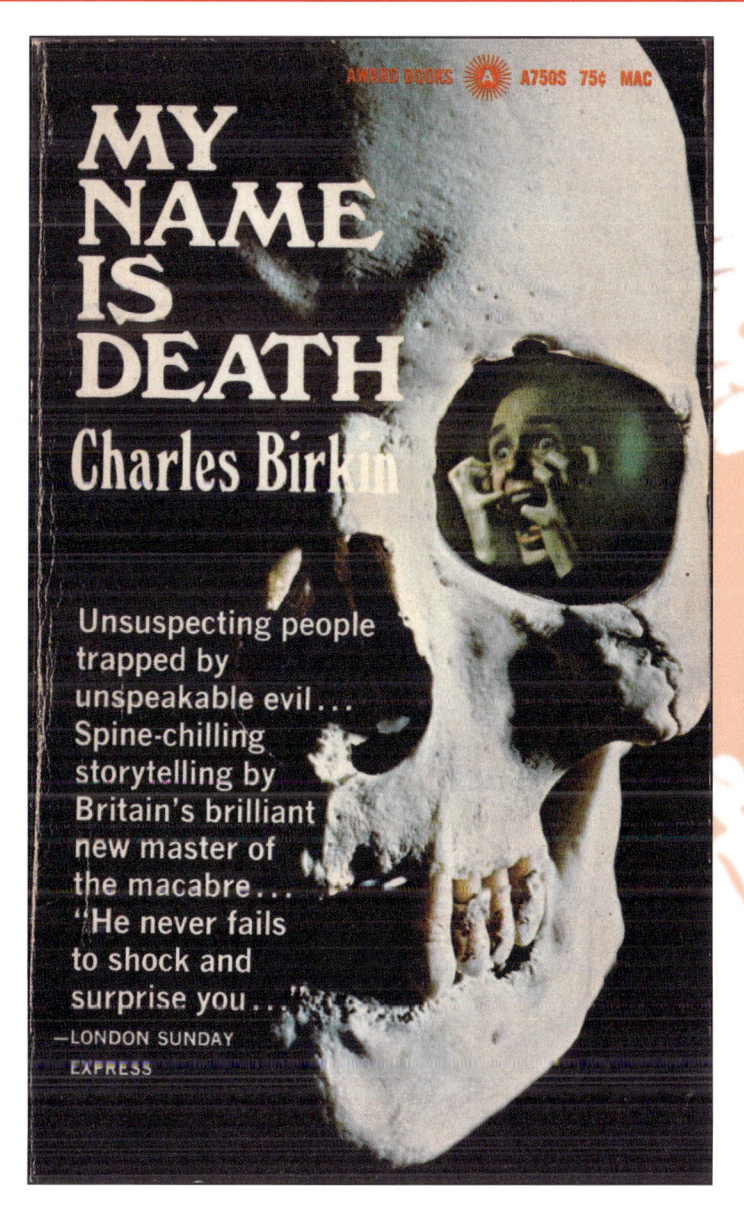

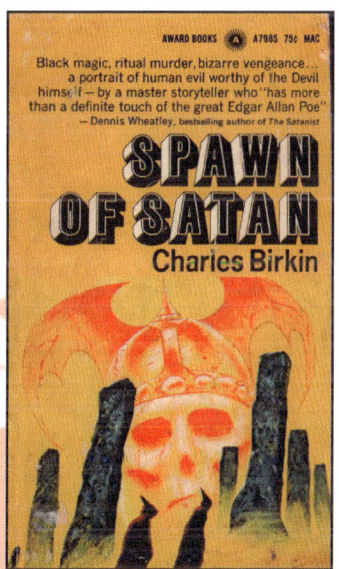

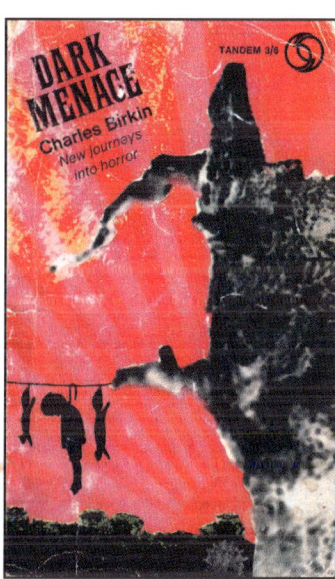

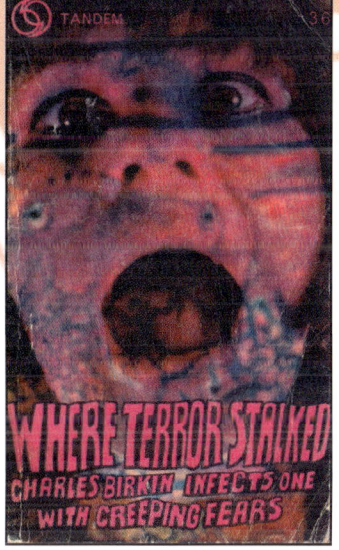

THE PAPERBACK FANTASTIC – HORROR

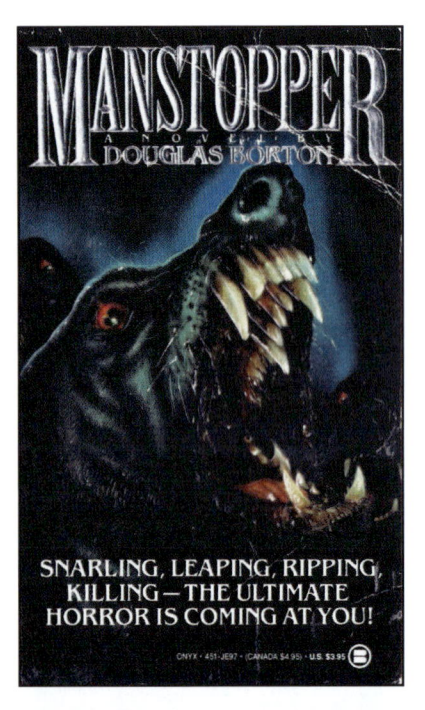

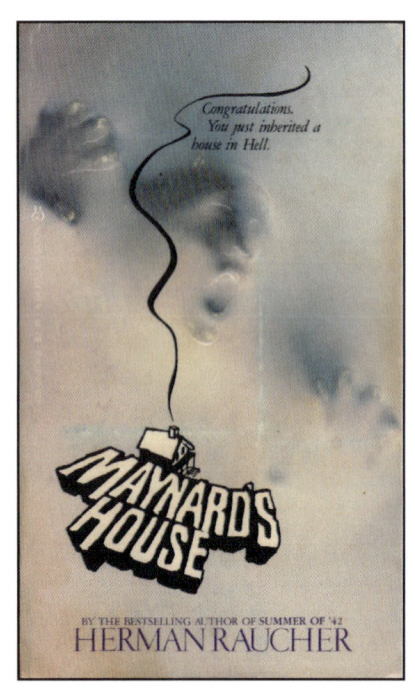

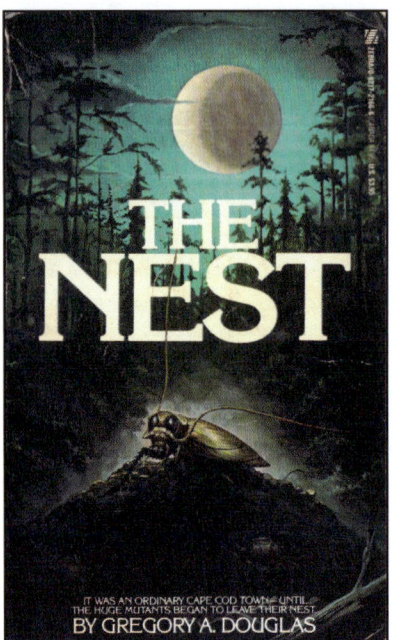

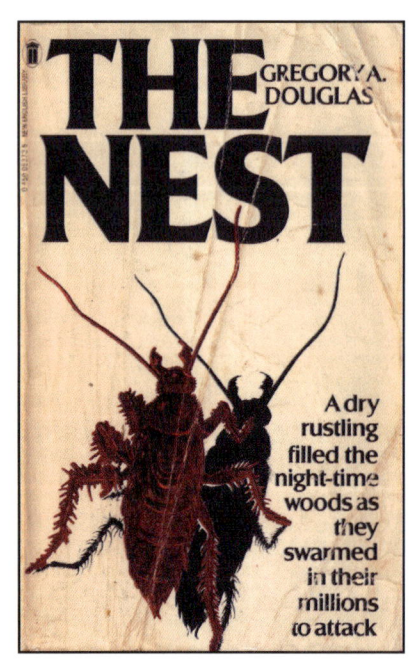

MANSTOPPER
The first of four horror novels carrying the credit of Douglas Borton.

MAYNARD'S HOUSE
Two editions of Rasucher's cult novel. 1981 paperback from Berkley and the 1980 hardback first edition with a cover by Wendell Minor.

THE NEST
Both the US and UK versions of Douglas' superior mutant cockroaches critter-horror are hard to find and received a welcome reprinting by Valancourt Books in 2019. Zebra US 1980 and UK New English Library 1982.

40

follows is an atmospheric—and somewhat claustrophobic—experience. *Maynard's House* is well thought of by many, and yet I can't help feeling I should like it more. All the elements are there for a top-notch horror novel: interesting characters and on-point dialogue, the perfect stage for inevitable mayhem, and a poetic and compelling style of writing which heightens the mood with each layered paragraph. Yet, while stylistically this novel deserves high marks, it leaves me wanting. No plot spoilers here . . . I will simply say the ending didn't justify the investment for me. There is plenty of impressive build-up but little in the way of actual action and resolution. Still, I give Raucher a great deal of credit for his use of evocative language and ability to compel the reader to soldier on. Despite the lack of much happening, we find ourselves unable to stop reading. We must learn whatever we can of the cabin's history; we must learn what is to ultimately become of Austin Fletcher. Will he go mad? Is he already mad and what he witnesses the result of delirium? Will the mythical beings said to haunt the woods make an appearance? Raucher's tale practically forces you to burn through the final pages in an effort to answer these and other questions, and herein lies the reason for the novel's cult following.

S. Clayton Rhodes

THE NEST
Gregory A. Douglas
1982

"A superior novel of this sort and well worth reading..."

The Nest is a far superior book to the author's other horror novel, *The Unholy Smile*. The style is quite different, with short sentences and chapters, which helps to produce a rollicking pace, and no superfluous characters and plotlines. It's a classic 'when animals attack' novel, this time with mutant cockroaches taking over idyllic Yarkie island off Cape Cod in the United States. The main character is Elizabeth Carr, a senior at Radcliffe College, who is visiting her grandfather Elias Johnson, the island's sheriff, with a Radcliffe friend named Bonnie Taylor. There are the usual set pieces, with various native islanders and visitors getting gruesomely dispatched, including a stoned punk who gets it into his head to masturbate in the loamy soil only to be shredded alive in the process.

These mutant insects are particularly nasty – they are much larger than the usual garden variety cockroaches, with large, grinding mandibles. They go for the eyes first and are able to completely obliterate a body by grinding flesh and bones and carting the remains off to the nest, a kind of pulsing 'brain' of millions of connected cockroaches that enables the cockroaches to operate as a single united entity, much like termites. Elias calls in Elizabeth's love interest, a Harvard biologist, Peter Hubbard, and his colleague, the beautiful Wanda Lindstrom. The author has done his homework and Hubbard and Lindstrom are the mouthpieces of some interesting entomological diatribes that don't much interrupt the flow of the story. After some lucky escapes, and a particularly nasty set piece where a bunch of islander children on an ill-conceived boat trip in rough seas are either drowned or eaten alive or both, the nest is seemingly dispatched. However, just when you think things have returned to normal, Elizabeth is threatened by a second nest, and Peter Hubbard must save the day. The novel was made into a 1988 film, produced by Roger Corman's wife, Julie, but the plot bares little relationship to the novel. A superior novel of this sort and well worth reading – the original paperback editions are difficult to find, but it was reprinted as the first in Valancourt's 'Paperbacks from Hell' series in 2019.

James Doig

NIGHT SHIFT
Stephen King
1978

"You can see the improvement in King's writing as you work your way through the book..."

King's first short story collection, largely made up of stories published in men's magazines such as **Cavalier**, **Gallery** and **Penthouse**, back when the joke that 'I only read them for the stories' actually had some truth to it. With stories spanning eight years, you can see the improvement in King's writing as you work your way through the book. While the early stories like 'Graveyard Shift', with the basement full of rats, or 'The Mangler', with the possessed steam press, bring the shocks and are entertaining, the later stories like 'Children of the Corn' or 'One for the Road', a follow-up to *Salem's Lot*, are classics. The book also contains a number of stories without any supernatural aspects but are still well worth reading. 'Quitter's Inc.', 'The Last Rung on the Ladder' and 'The Ledge', the premise of which was used by Alan Moore for a chapter of **V for Vendetta**, keep the reader involved from the start. My only complaint is the sequence of the stories, as the last story is the non-supernatural 'The Woman in the Room'. In it, a son deals with his mother's end-of-life issues. It is a powerful story, and very depressing. Personally, I wished the book ended with monsters or ghosts or some other supernatural creatures, rather than something actually horrifying, like a terminally ill parent. Still, this is a top-notch collection of stories from a master storyteller.

Tom Tesarek

NIGHTSHADES AND DAMNATIONS
Gerald Kersh
1968

"A feast of wonderful material to be savoured..."

A collection of eleven stories of "the weird, the unspeakable, the bizarre", collected from magazines as varied as **The Strand**, **The Saturday Evening Post** (for the most part), **Esquire** and **Playboy**. It's a relatively small sampling of Kersh's work, which by the time of his death in 1968 ran to over 75 short stories and 20 novels. But it is a feast of wonderful material to be savoured, as Kersh takes on the role of barroom raconteur, charming his audience with stories which are fabulous, ridiculous, horrifying, humorous and full of pathos. 'The Queen of Pig Island' has four members of a circus washed up on a desert island, with the limbless matriarch finding herself in a love triangle with a slow-witted strongman and twin midgets. Ludicrous and in bad taste, Kersh somehow manages to make it touching. 'Men Without Bones' is a classic twist tale that should be called 'Men with Bones', with titular creatures that should be comical yet are revolting and skin-crawling. And as for the punch-line... Perhaps there are elements of Kersh to be found in Karmesin, the rascal who claims to count millionaires and royalty as his friends yet wraps the scraps from his plate in a handkerchief and squirrels them away, a wonderful comic invention who had me reading 'Bone for Debunkers' with a smile on my face.

Justin Marriott

AN ODOUR OF DECAY
Martin Jenson
1975

"Sufficient confidence ... to slip in some sly humour..."

Martin Jenson produced a trio of slim yet interesting horror books for UK publishers New English Library (NEL) before disappearing off the radar, with this being his most enjoyable. Three sisters get more than they bargained for when they move into an inherited mansion and are possessed by a malevolent spirit. The eldest sister Belinda experiences sudden strange attacks of epilepsy, Sarah the youngest develops a craving for sexual perversion and Nan is infected with a morbid obsession with death, all characteristics of the house-bound and smallpox infected teenage boy who had committed suicide in their house in the previous century. It's up to Belinda's beau Terence to break the spell and save the sisters from the powers of the vengeful dead. Great fun is to be had with this effective page-turner, which in pace and tone is reminiscent of one of NEL's pulp classics, Guy Smith's *The Sucking Pit*. Jenson may lack the lurid sensibilities of Smith and be more gothic in his approach, but on this evidence is more than capable of giving the great scribbler a run for his money. Particularly in the case of Sarah, the bookworm turned sex-fiend, whose kinky activities will make any male's eyes water! Jenson offers more than a Smith-clone, with his intelligence shining through in the book's interesting theories as to the nature of possession and hauntings and showing sufficient confidence as a writer to slip in some sly humour. *Justin Marriott*

NIGHTSHADES AND DAMNATIONS The presence of Leo and Diane Dillon's distinctive woodcut style art on the cover was at the request of Harlan Ellison who edited this collection.

AN ODOUR OF DECAY Martin Jenson's slim yet interesting book was deserving of a better cover than this rather generic image from New English Library.

NIGHT SHIFT At the opposite end of the spectrum was Don Brautigam's brilliant image for this King anthology, which has become a classic, spawning various homages across wider pop culture.

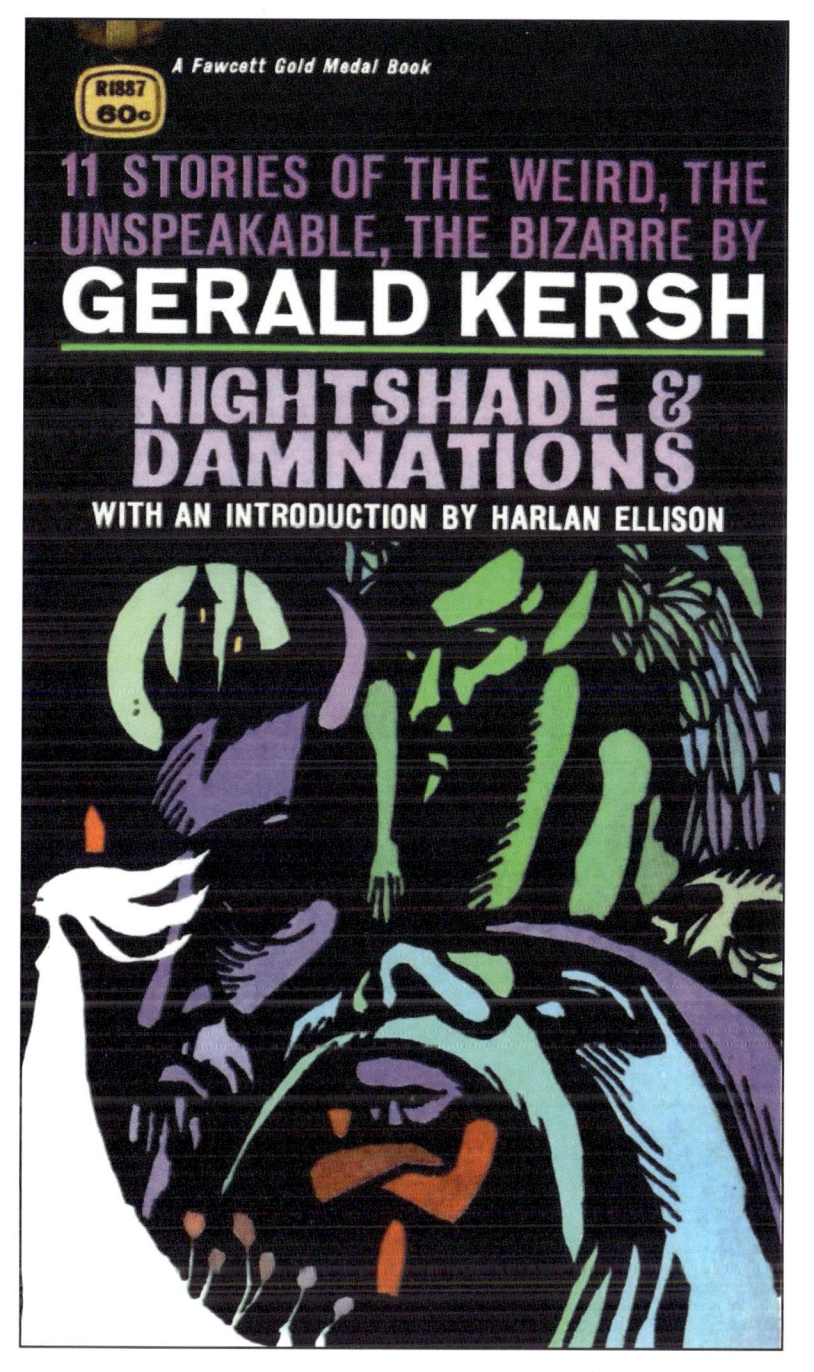

A Fawcett Gold Medal Book

R1887 60¢

11 STORIES OF THE WEIRD, THE UNSPEAKABLE, THE BIZARRE BY
GERALD KERSH
NIGHTSHADE & DAMNATIONS
WITH AN INTRODUCTION BY HARLAN ELLISON

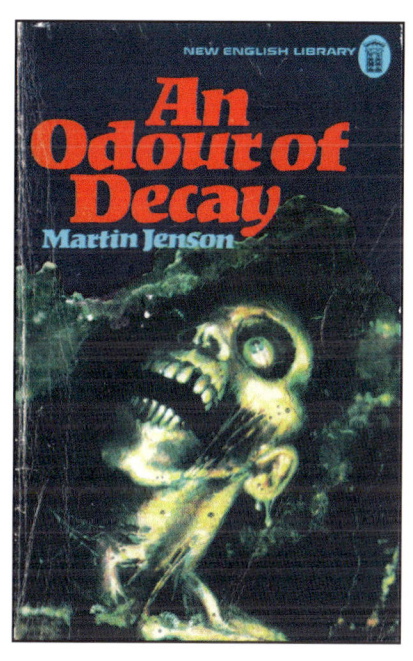

NEW ENGLISH LIBRARY

An Odour of Decay
Martin Jenson

SIGNET • 451 • E9746 • $2.95

BY THE AUTHOR OF
THE DEAD ZONE & FIRESTARTER
STEPHEN KING
NIGHT SHIFT
EXCURSIONS INTO HORROR

THE PAPERBACK FANTASTIC — HORROR

THE OFFSPRING
J N Williamson
1984

"A mutant-daughter blessed with heightened psychic powers..."

Another one of those obscenely wealthy industrialist types is using his money to indulge his whims, this one in pursuit of creating the perfect daughter. What would possibly go wrong? Central to the book is a theory that some of the Ancient Egyptians were part of a superior but short-lived branch of human evolution. Following the discovery of an intact womb in a literal Mummy made of one of the super-humans, a mutant-daughter blessed with heightened psychic powers is spawned. Lovecraft's 'The Dunwich Horror' with a dash of *The Omen*, relocated to the millionaire's condos of upscale Manhattan, *The Offspring* is well-written and has a certain zip, but the hokey premise is totally undone by the final chapter reveal of the monstrous daughter, which perhaps was better off staying out of sight in the tradition of Lovecraft.
Justin Marriott

RAZORBACK
Peter Brennan
1984

"The razorback boar plays only a bit part..."

I've got two editions of *Razorback* published by the British publisher, Fontana. The first is the 1982 edition with a cover by celebrated British artist John Holmes, and the second is the movie tie-in published in 1984 with cover art by well-known Australian artist and graphic designer, Brian Clinton. The second is scarcer and probably more desirable as movie tie-ins tend to be. This is one of those rare occasions where the movie is far better than the book it was based on. Peter Brennan's novel is way too long and combines too many plot threads, including a completely irrelevant diamond smuggling operation being run out of a pet food factory, PetPak. The main story line concerns the disappearance of Beth Winters, an investigative journalist who gets too close to the criminal activities of PetPak. In fact, she has been gang raped and left to die in the remote New South Wales outback where she is killed and eaten by the huge razorback boar of the title. Beth's sister, Ginny, and Beth's estranged husband, Gene Taylor, who are former lovers, attempt to find her. Also in the mix is Jake Cullen, a professional hunter whose son was eaten by a massive razorback and who nobody believes – he is clearly a type of obsessive Captain Ahab figure. Prefacing some of the chapters in italics is the story of a kangaroo attempting to outrun the razorback that is hunting it and their interactions with human beings along the way, including Beth Winters and Jake Cullen. What ties the disparate threads together is the theme of the environment and its destruction – a man-made drought has caused the razorback to travel south from Queensland in search of food, kangaroos are an endangered species caused by culling and hunting, unscrupulous industries are stripping the land bare. In all of this, the razorback boar plays only a bit part until near the end of the book when it takes centre stage as Gene Taylor fights for his life. Whereas the novel might be described as an eco-thriller, the film is unashamedly a horror film, and with all its faults, something of a cult classic. Peter Brennan, known primarily as the creator and producer of *Judge Judy*, authored another novel called *Sudden Impact* (1978) evidently a tennis themed thriller of no great merit, not to be confused with the later Dirty Harry movie. *James Doig*

SABAT
Guy N Smith
4 books, 1982-83

"Exactly the dour and unbending individual you imagine a real-life vigilante type to be..."

Soldier-of-fortune turned occult ass-kicker Mark Sabat, battled the forces of evil across four books: *The Graveyard Vultures* (1982), *The Blood Merchants* (1982), *Cannibal Cult* (1982) and *The Druid Connection* (1983). Having been expelled from boarding school, defrocked as a priest and court-martialled out of the SAS (not a track record that suggests a sunny disposition and an ability to make friends), Sabat's mission to defeat the occult begins when he hunts down his brother Quentin, a man so evil he's known as 'Satan's Henchman.' Although Sabat kills his brother during their final confrontation, Quentin transfers part of his evil soul into Sabat, meaning the man is destined to fighting the forces of evil internally as well as externally. Breathlessly paced, inventive and dripping with atmosphere, the original quadrology of

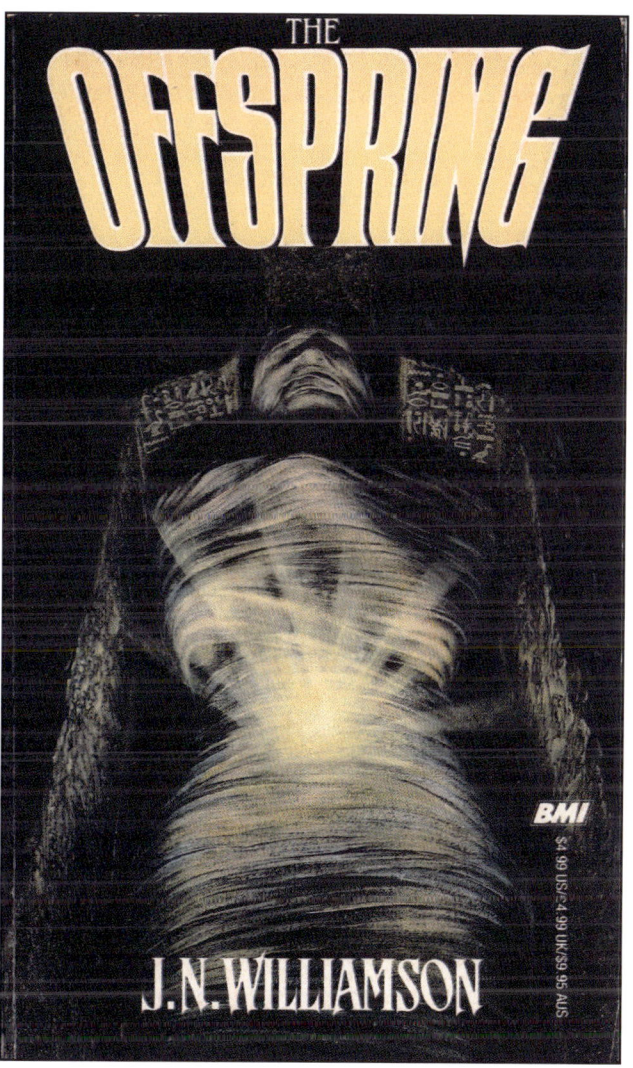

RAZORBACK
Brennan's 1981 story was adapted to film in 1984, gaining a cult following and several film tie-in editions. Featured is Fontana UK's tie-in from 1984, who also published the first edition in 1981.

THE OFFSPRING
A solitary printing for the prolific Williamson's melding of The Mummy and the then popular, demon kid genres.

Sabat adventures are without doubt Guy Smith's best work in the pulp fiction field. As well as being gritty and nihilistic, with Sabat being exactly the dour and unbending individual you imagine a real-life vigilante type to be, the writing is peppered with Smith's trademark idiosyncrasies such as Sabat being a compulsive masturbator! Relatively easy to track down in their NEL editions, an omnibus of the books was issued by Creation Books under the title *Dead Meat* in 1996 with the addition of two short stories, and due to a printing error which slashed the print run, is very difficult to track down.
Justin Marriott

THE SAXONBURY PRINTOUT
Phil Smith
1979

"A 70s horror thriller with a mordant atmosphere and a cerebral core..."

An example of quiet horror and possibly the (over-used term ahoy) folk horror genres, *The Saxonbury Printout* will likely have been too ahead of its time in the late 70s as the publishing world flocked to the 'animals attack' genre but is dated now due to its story hinging on a cutting-edge super-computer. When an American couple relocate to the English countryside as her computer scientist husband lands a plum job, the bored and dislocated wife immerses herself into the local history. She discovers she now lives on the site of a Viking slaughter of the Saxon villagers who were mass-buried in a hill (hence the name Saxon-bury), many alive, and her obsession with this incident culminates in her husband using the computer to recreate events in a simulation exercise. What could be possibly go wrong? You'll need to make it through 100-odd of the 130 pages to find out, but Smith just about kept me hanging in there to find out, with a series of eccentric characters such as the curator of a dust-covered local museum, and unsettling images such as a carpet of craneflies with their wings and legs bitten off by wasps and the brutish treatment by his co-workers of a young man with learning difficulties. A 70s horror thriller with a mordant atmosphere and a cerebral core, presumably its key inspiration was *The Stone Tapes* a BBC TV play from 1972 written by Nigel *Quatermass* Kneale. It also reminded me of John Blackburn's *Children of the Night*, which is a compliment, but is short of being a recommended read.
Justin Marriott

THE SCARLET BOY
Arthur Calder-Marshall
1962

"Accomplished writing and the careful unveiling of events..."

Contemporary reviews compared this novel to *The Turn of the Screw*, and while it is certainly literary supernatural fiction, it is more clearly a Christian fantasy like *The Exorcist* or *The Case Against Satan* but without the histrionics. The narrator, George Grantley is a historian who has lived his entire life in the small English town of Wilchester. He is approached by his friend, a successful London-based lawyer named Kit Everness, to find a house for him and his family in town, preferably one in a run-down condition that his wife Nieves, a Spanish artist, can do up. They have a young daughter, Rosa, who is a boarder at a local school, St Clair's, but she hates boarding and buying a house locally will allow her to attend as a day girl. Grantley discovers that a place he knew well as a child, Anglesey House, may be available. Now an uninhabited shell, Grantley used to play there with a childhood friend, Charles Scarlet. Following Charles's untimely death, Grantley would regularly visit Charles's glamorous mother, Helen, who treated him as a surrogate son. Everness purchases the house, but along the way Grantley discovers that Anglesey house is believed to be haunted and subsequent research reveals not only that Charles committed suicide, but that another boy, Peter Inglesey, had committed suicide on the same day several centuries before. Grantley realises that ancient evil entities possessed the children and that Rosa's life is at risk. Grantley's

THE SAXONBURY PRINTOUT Smith also wrote the tie-in to *The Incredible Melting Man*, which was only printed in the UK.

THE SCARLET BOY Josh Kirby shows the influence of Richard Powers on his early work.

SABAT 2: THE BLOOD MERCHANTS All four of the NEL published Sabats employed the same cover motif, including a gold coloured leaf for the logo.

The Paperback Fantastic - Horror

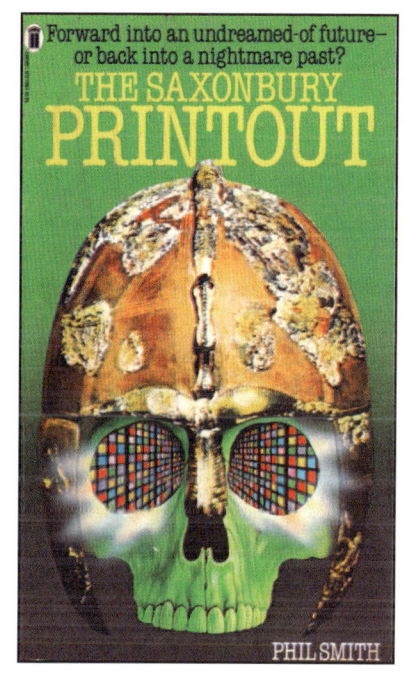

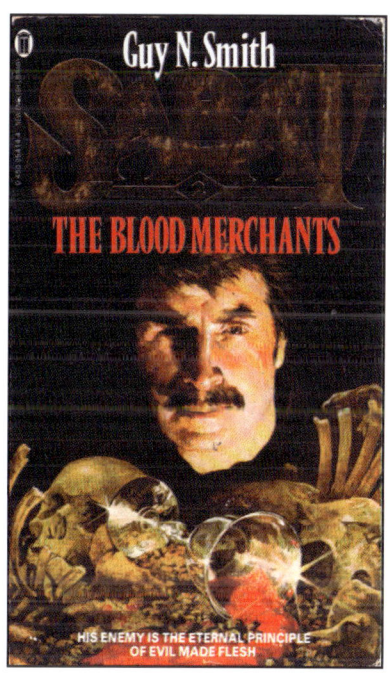

FANTASTIC FOCUS 5

THE SATAN SLEUTH

THE SATAN SLEUTH: NO.1 FALLEN ANGEL
Michael Avallone
1974

"A quick read with plenty of interesting cultural references..."

Michael Avallone was an incredibly prolific author who wrote over two hundred paperback titles across the horror, spy, private eye and gothic genres and a swathe of television tie-ins, including for **The Partridge Family**. Best known as the author of the **Ed Noon** PI series, Avallone also tried his hand at Satanic fiction with the short-lived Satan Sleuth series. *Fallen Angel* is the first of the three-book series and is essentially an origin story. It details how the fabulously wealthy and ultra-fit adventurer Philip St. George becomes "a crusader against The Evil One and all his minions on earth", following the slaughter of his wife by devil worshippers. There is not a lot to this book. Most of the first half is taken up with lengthy internal monologues by St. George, and some veiled descriptions of the horrific acts performed on his wife by four "really sick, demented, half-mad creatures from another planet." After the slaughter, the four killers, known as Wolfman, Doc, Dracula and Baby Jane, hole up in a cave not too far from St. George's mansion, before returning to the scene of the crime where the 'Satan Sleuth' is waiting for them with a secret stash of weapons. The final confrontation is rather bland and muted but does set the scene for the subsequent books in the series. *Fallen Angel* is not a great book, but it is a quick read with plenty of interesting cultural references from the early 1970s. It is also extremely dated in its attitudes.

Jeff Popple
☠☠

THE GENERAL INTEREST IN THE OCCULT IN THE 70S GAVE BIRTH TO A SHORT-LIVED NUMBER OF OCCULT DETECTIVES, INCLUDING THE SATAN SLEUTH

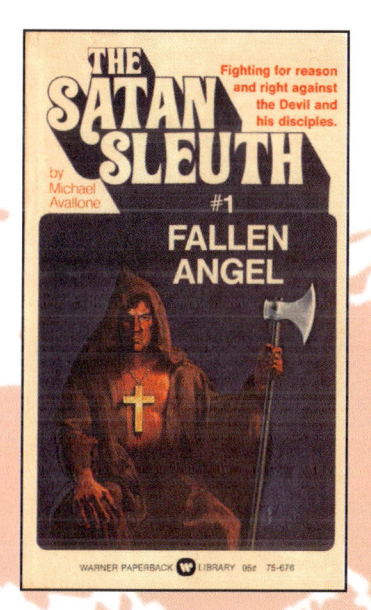

There were three Satan Sleuth novels published - *Fallen Angel* (1974), *The Werewolf Stalks Tonight* (1975) and *Devil, Devil* (1975). Covers by Charles Sovak. Apparently there were two further novels planned by author Avallone - *Vampires Wild* and *Zombie Depot* - but they never saw publication as Warner had no interest in continuing the series. Two were reprinted in the UK by the short-lived 'series imprint' MEWS Books, with excellent Tony Masero covers.

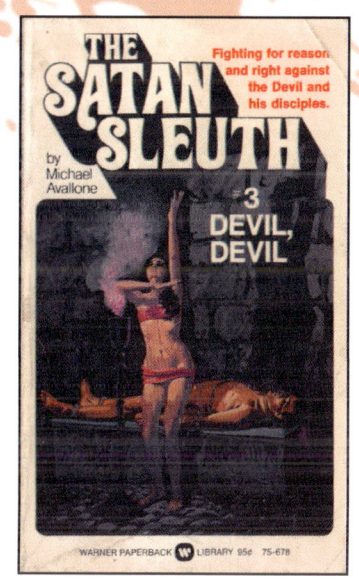

The Paperback Fantastic – Horror

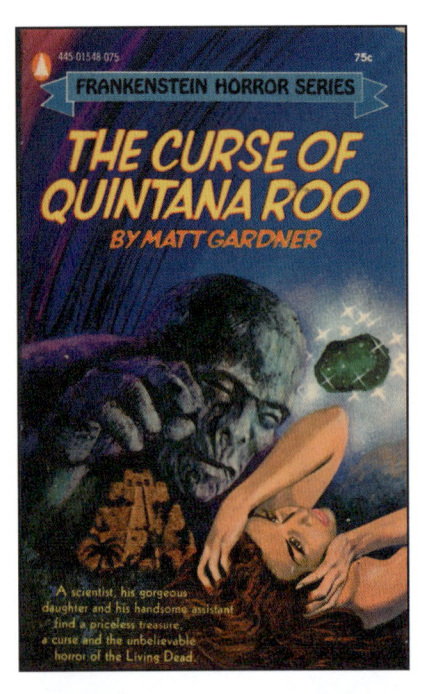

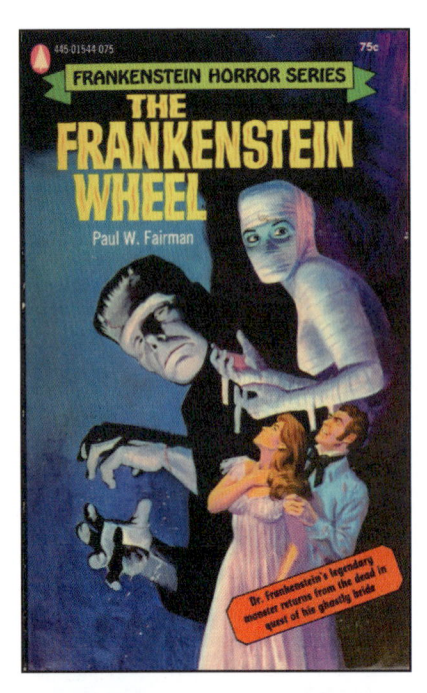

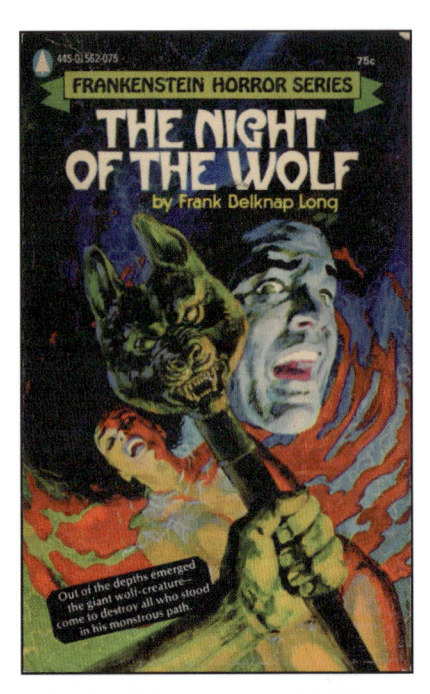

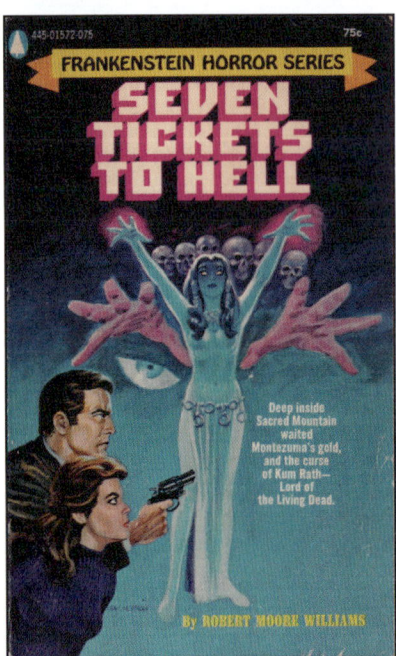

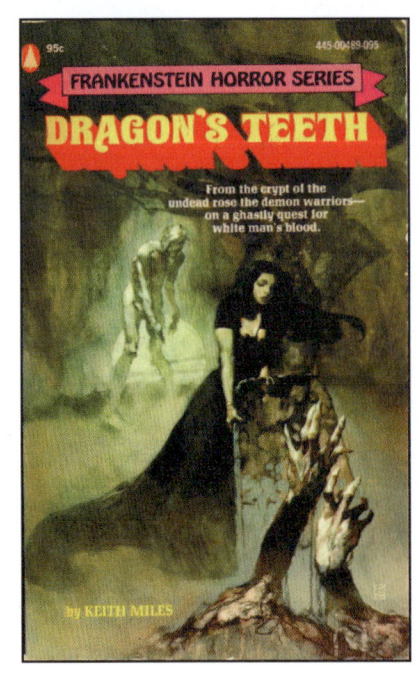

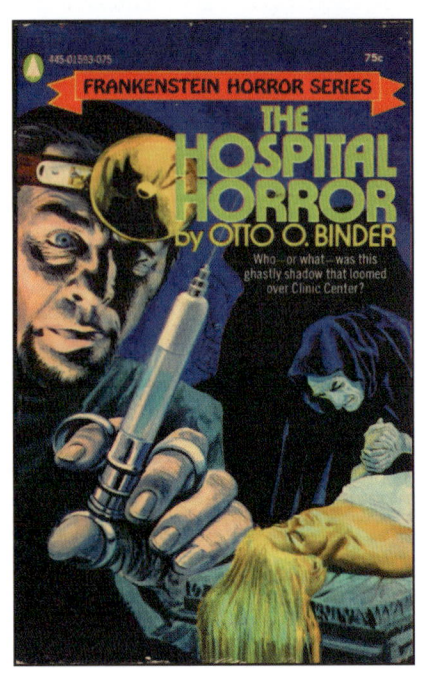

Frankenstein Horror Series

- **The Curse of Quintana Roo** by Matt Gardner
  A scientist, his gorgeous daughter and his handsome assistant find a priceless treasure, a curse and the unbelievable horror of the Living Dead.

- **The Frankenstein Wheel** by Paul W. Fairman
  Dr. Frankenstein's legendary monster returns from the dead in quest of his ghastly bride.

- **The Night of the Wolf** by Frank Belknap Long
  Out of the depths emerged the giant wolf-creature come to destroy all who stood in his monstrous path.

- **Seven Tickets to Hell** by Robert Moore Williams
  Deep inside Sacred Mountain waited Montezuma's gold, and the curse of Kum Rath—Lord of the Living Dead.

- **Dragon's Teeth** by Keith Miles
  From the crypt of the undead rose the demon warriors—on a ghastly quest for white man's blood.

- **The Hospital Horror** by Otto O. Binder
  Who—or what—was this ghastly shadow that loomed over Clinic Center?

50

faith enables him to see that an exorcism is needed to free the house and Rosa from the demonic forces at work, though he has a hard time convincing his strongly rationalist friend, Everness. Christian apologetics intrude occasionally, but the accomplished writing and the careful unveiling of events leading to an effective climax make up for it.
James Doig

and a group of treasure hunters, who believe the lost gold of Cortez is in the area. Oh yeah, did I mention the zombies, invisibility, VTOL aircraft, and ancient gods? It's quite an interesting storyline but becomes stilted and awkward under the constraints of the author's chosen literary device. A shame actually, as this should have been a lot better.
Scott Ranalli

SEVEN TICKETS TO HELL
Robert Moore Williams
1972

"Stilted and awkward under the constraints of the author's chosen literary device…"

From the Frankenstein Horror Series, which was a series of nine from new and established PB pulpsters. Things started weird right out of the gate, when I found that the author had chosen Second Person Singular to tell this tale. This was quite awkward but got somewhat less so as the book went on. The chapters alternate between the viewpoints of two main characters, a federal narcotics agent, and a top-level scientist on sabbatical at his second home in rural Central Mexico. The narcotics agent is following a heroin distribution chain; he meets a local girl who becomes the mysterious femme fatale of the story. The scientist is relaxing when he finds he must come to the aid of an old native brujo, or medicine man, that he has befriended; the brujo has a young girl in tow and they are on the run from religious fanatics. Both storylines draw inexorably towards the Sacred Mountain, the subject of many local legends. There are additional factors including the Mafia

SHADES OF EVIL
Hugh B Cave
1982

"The horror elements are somewhat subdued by today's standards…"

There is something coming from the lake. It looks like a foggy blob at first but then coalesces into the shape of a human woman. First, two large dogs are found dead, but later, residents of the nearby condominium complex start to be killed. Will Platt is an author of occult stories who lives in the complex and he feels there is some connection to his soon-to-be ex-wife as well as a recent trip to Jamaica. Voodoo certainly has something to do with all of it. Hugh B. Cave was a prolific pulpster, selling over 800 stories during the 1920's and 30's in just about every genre imaginable. He was probably known best for his horror and weird menace stories, and this novel is a good example of that. The story is told in three parts with the first and third taking place in Florida near the aforementioned lake while the third is a flashback to the island of Jamaica. Interestingly, the author, after a stint in WW2 as a war correspondent, moved to Jamaica and managed a coffee plantation while continuing his writing career. This has resulted in accurate and insightful descriptions of the island and its inhabitants in this novel. I was surprised to discover the novel reads much more like a modern horror story than a pulp story. It's much like something from Dean Koontz or John Saul. While I've never been a big fan of voodoo in novels, it works well in this book. Good thing because there is a lot of it here, as well as other occult practices that I am not familiar with like obeah and bocorism. I guess that prevalence is not surprising considering the author's time in Haiti resulted in his publishing *Haiti Highroad to Adventure*, a nonfiction work that some claim is the "best report on voodoo in English." The man knew his subject. Many of the main characters in this

THE FRANKENSTEIN HORROR SERIES

Pictured on the opposite page are six of the nine entries to this series which had no continuity or link between entries, other than its banner and artist Gray Morrow producing 8 of the covers (with the exception of *Dragon's Teeth* which was painted by Catherine Jeffrey Jones). Published by Popular Library from 1972 to 1973, the series has become collectible, with some titles especially rare due to the poor quality of their binding which makes them vulnerable to falling apart.

novel not only believe in the associated powers but seem to take it for granted that others do too. And they do! Nobody ever really questions the occult nature of the mysterious apparition, and easily buy into the premise. In general, the horror elements are somewhat subdued by today's standards, but it does focus on the fear and apprehension aspects rather than any kind of gore and blood splatter.
Benjamin Thomas

THE SLIME BEAST
Guy N Smith
1976

"I can only imagine the wry smile as she would hand-over the latest typed up pages of masticated brains and rutting protagonists..."

Unrestrained and following a logic of its very own (some would say, from another planet), this slim and rough-hewn novel reads as if Smith discovered a script for an unmade monster movie of the 1950s and gleefully updated it with his trademark gusto. Freed from its resting place by intrepid but incompetent archaeologists, alien-tourist the Slime Beast goes on a bloody rampage until stopped in its tracks by a homemade flamethrower. Smith gleefully provides nauseatingly detailed descriptions of the beast's eating habits, such as using its long sliver of a yellow tongue to lick the pulped brains out of splintered skulls. Trademark Smith-isms abound, with poachers being the midnight snack of choice for the beast, the heroes besieged in a handy hide-out, and the threat of impending death bringing on sexual abandon and a worrying disregard for contraception. Apparently, we have British institution Midland Bank to thank for *The Slime Beast*. At that time Smith was working on a van delivering cash to local bank branches, and during the considerable downtime, would furiously scribble his latest novel on Midland bank headed paper. On the way home, Smith would drop off his hand-written notes to a friend and over-night she would type them up for collection the next day. I can only imagine the wry smile as she would hand-over the latest typed up pages of masticated brains and rutting protagonists.
Justin Marriott

SOME OF YOUR BLOOD
Theodore Sturgeon
1961

"No bats, fog, or creaking coffin lids in this tale..."

To say *Some of Your Blood* is a unique entry in the vampire sub-genre of horror would be an understatement. Forget Bela Lugosi and his crimson-lined cape, skip Christopher Lee and his flaming contact lenses and ivory plastic fangs, it's time to meet . . . uh, George Smith? Okay, the name of the vampire may raise an eyebrow, but get past that and you'll be in for a vampiric treat. Much of this tight little masterpiece's appeal is that it presents itself as a case file of a real live vampire. It details an autobiographical account of George, a soldier whose life began in abject poverty, and who was eventually led to vampirism of a sort. No spoilers here other than you can bet there will be no bats, fog, or creaking coffin lids in this tale; it is no Gothic supernatural tale—and it is all the more chilling for that fact! Sturgeon's writing here is rich, the realism is edgy, and the choice of how the story unfolds (again, as an authentic case file, courtesy of one Dr. Outerbridge) is inspiring. And there is a hummer of a reveal at one point that will knock you for a loop. At less than one hundred and fifty pages, *Some of Your Blood* is a quick read, so you have no excuse to skip this often overlooked and somewhat forgotten gem if you've not read it before. For me, it ranks as one of my top favourite vampire novels, and I promise you I've read many.
S Clayton Rhodes

TALES OF LOVE AND HORROR
Don Congdon
1961

"There isn't a clunker to be found in this selection..."

An early, if not the first, example of the "scared stiff" genre which mixed sex with horror. Congdon was evidently something of a rake as he also delivered two other collections of literary erotica for Ballantine Books. There isn't a clunker to be found in this selection, although there is a certain sameness (stories typically fall into the EC twist tale of one spurned lover taking revenge upon another) which makes it a selection to dip into rather than read in one sitting. Stand outs are Davis Grubb's 'Horsehair Trunk' an account of astral

THE SLIME BEAST
The 1976 and first edition of Smith's rambunctious and gleefully outrageous SF horror. The cover art is uncredited, but possibly painted by Ray Feibush in his energetic and colourful style.

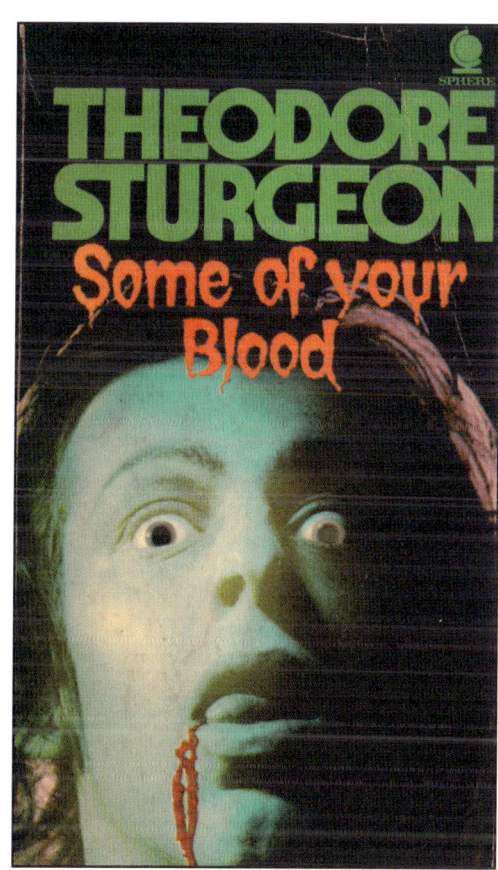

SOME OF YOUR BLOOD
Sturgeon's genre-bending novel is difficult to classify, perhaps reflected by this garish and hackneyed photo chosen by Sphere UK for this 1967 edition.

THE PAPERBACK FANTASTIC - HORROR

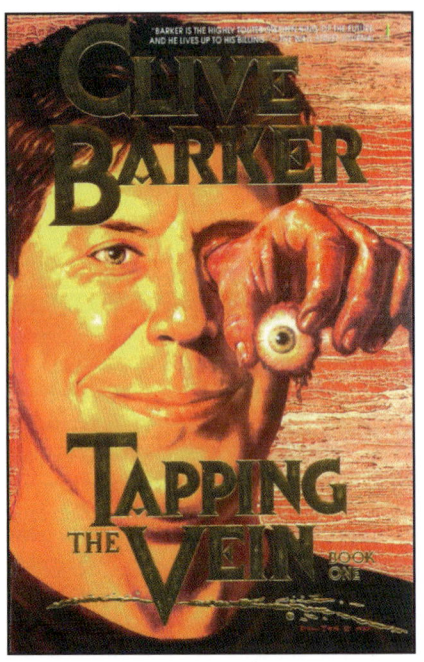

54

projection with a twist that I didn't not see materialising, and Richard Matheson's 'No Such Thing as a Vampire' which is a classic to grace any anthology. It was Robert Graves' 'The Shout' that truly seduced me, a sophisticated and honest account of a couple's relationship with an unreliable narrator who admits to changing the story each time he tells it. Breath-taking. Congdon, and his son, later joined up to pull together *Alone by Night* which was a very decent monster-themed selection.

Justin Marriott

TAPPING THE VEIN VOLUME ONE
Eclipse Comics
1989

"Key themes from Barker's original were missing..."

As Clive Barker became the hottest name in horror, and with English language comics searching for an adult audience, it was a natural step to adapt Barker's stories into comic strip format. Putting the graphic into graphic novels, **Tapping the Vein** ran for 5 issues, each adapting two of Barker's short stories across 52 pages, on higher quality paper and with sharper reproduction than typical of comics. It may be stating the obvious, but I am reviewing the comics rather than the original stories by Barker. Neither story were obvious choices to kick off a commercial comic in the late 80s, as 'Human Remains' main character is a bisexual gigolo who is coveted by an animated statue with the ability to imitate, and 'Pig Blood Blues' features a disgraced policeman seeking redemption by working in a remand home for teenage boys. Of the two, 'Human Remains' is the more successful, with writer/artist P Craig Russell adroitly capturing the beauty and decay essential to the story's themes and using a variety of story-telling techniques to prevent a considered and darkly humorous story becoming static when committed to comic form. 'Pig Blood Blues', written by Chuck Wagner and Fred Burke and illustrated by Scott Hampton, is much less satisfactory. That it took two writers to adapt someone else's story over 22 pages was a warning sign, and I think key themes from Barker's original – which seems to evoke a strong reaction in readers – were missing, either intentionally due to their taboo nature, or because the team adapting it, failed to pick up on them. Hampton is an artist who can paint, but his lack of background detail and insistence on dressing the juveniles like extras from *Mad Max* means the story doesn't have any grounding in the gritty reality of a prison which is required as counterbalance for the more fantastical sequences. Overall, this is a quality package and I'll revisit others as I see them, but this debut issue can't be especially recommended.

Justin Marriott

TO THE DEVIL - A DAUGHTER
Dennis Wheatley
1953

"Manages the difficult task of making the horror seem almost plausible and grounded in reality..."

Thriller writer Molly Fountain is curious about Christina, the young girl who is her new next-door neighbour - a nice girl whose behaviour changes completely by night into a drunken gambling addict. She investigates and realizes that she has come across a case of demonic possession and that a group of Satanists have a terrible fate in store for the poor woman. Molly is determined to save the victim somehow, so she calls in help from her old boss in the British Secret Service and also from her son, John. (You can probably guess what happens when John meets Christina...) Dennis Wheatley's book begins as a mystery, transforms into an action/adventure novel and then descends into horror. Wheatley is very adept at ringing the changes seamlessly, and his research into Satanism was detailed and accurate. He manages the difficult task of making

---

TALES OF LOVE AND HORROR ORIGINAL ART
Richard Powers's surreal art for the 1961 Ballantine anthology, which like much of his work requires a bit of effort to reveal the themes in the image.

TAPPING THE VEIN ISSUE ONE
John Bolton provided an eye-grabbing portrait of Clive Barker for the first issue of this high-quality forum for adaptations of Barker's work.

HUMAN REMAINS
P Craig Russell's art for his contribution to **Tapping the Vein**, showcasing a variety of story-telling devices to maximise the opportunities the comics format in adapting prose stories.

FANTASTIC FOCUS 6

DRAC IS BACK!

WITH THE RESURGENCE OF SERIES FICTION KICKED OFF BY 'THE EXECUTIONER' MEN'S ADVENTURE CHARACTER IN THE EARLY 70S, BOOK PACKAGER LYLE KENYON ENGEL WOULD SHOP AROUND CONCEPTS FOR SERIES OF BOOKS, COMMITTING TO PUBLISHERS THE DELIVERY OF BOMB-PROOF MANUSCRIPTS FROM PROFESSIONAL WRITERS THEY COULD IMMEDIATELY PUT INTO PRINT UNDER PSEUDONYMS.

Robert Lory was chosen by Engel to write a new Dracula series, which originally saw print in Pinnacle in nine books between 1973 and 1975, of which NEL reprinted the first two in 1973 and then one a year until 1977.

Damien Harmon's career as a no-nonsense police officer comes to a brutal end when he is crippled by thugs. Confined to a wheelchair and with a steel plate in his skull which prevents his mind from being read, Harmon is committed to continuing the fight against crime. Using his considerable wealth and intellect, Harmon becomes an expert in the paranormal and heads off to Transylvania to resurrect Count Dracula. Implanting a silver stake in his The Lord of the Vampires chest with which he can trigger with his psychic powers, Harmon forces Dracula to join him in his crime-crushing crusade.

Lory dishes out some wild blending of genres, touching on the Manson cult in *Hand of Dracula*, voodoo in *Drums of Dracula* (undoubtedly inspired by the successful Bond film *Live and Let Die*), the Bathory legend in *The Witching of Dracula*. Wildly leftfield and imaginative, variable in their quality and scarred by their production-line ethos, these books must be the most bizarre in Dracula's history and are more fun to collect than read.

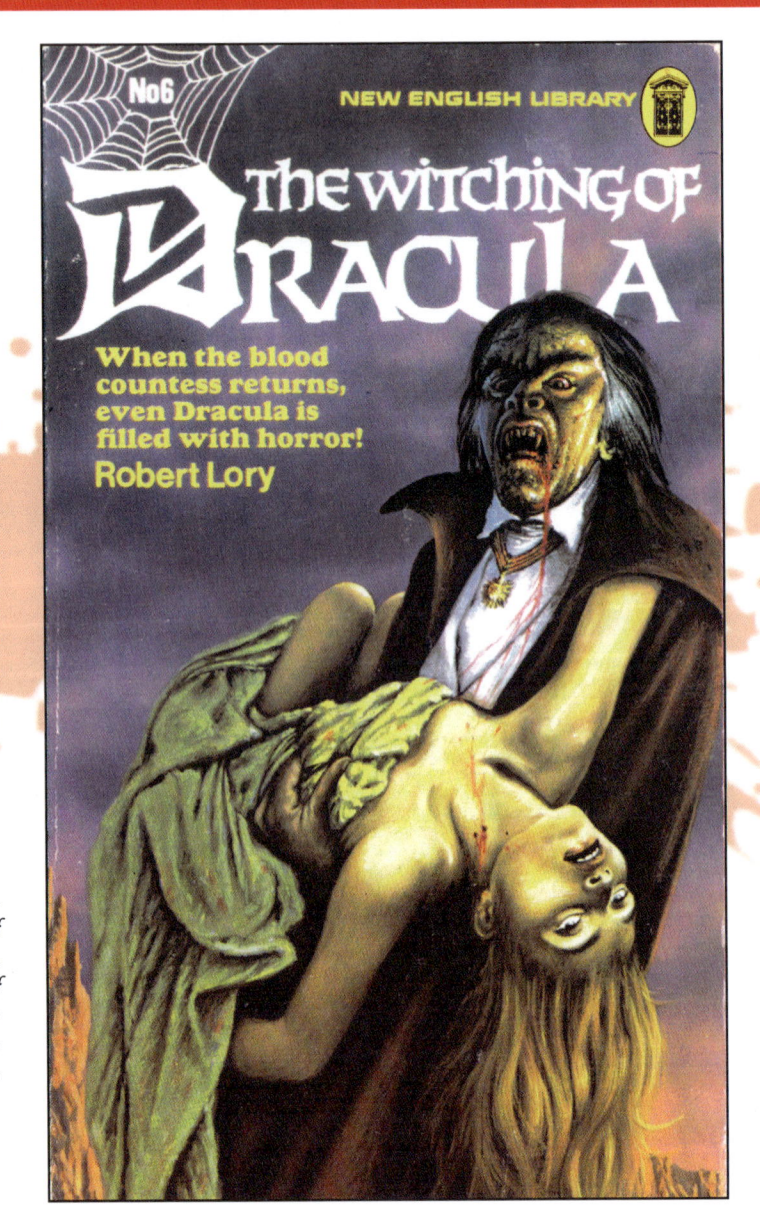

DRACULA RECEIVED HIS OWN SERIES OF NEW ADVENTURES IN THE 1970S, WRITTEN BY ROBERT LORY FOR BOOK PACKAGER LYLE KENYON ENGEL

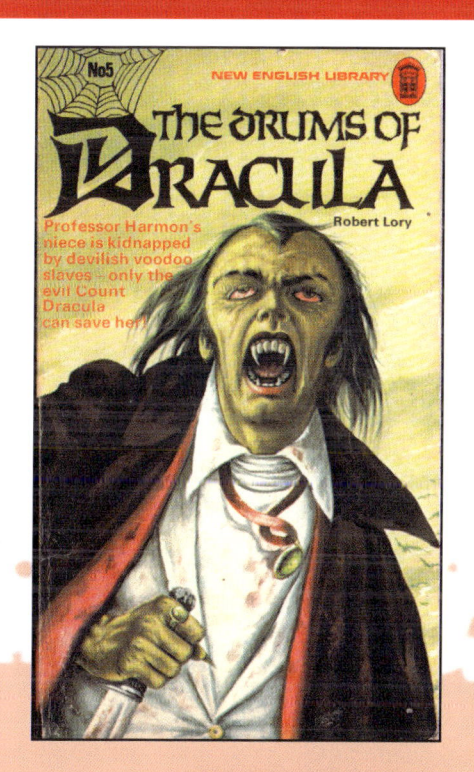

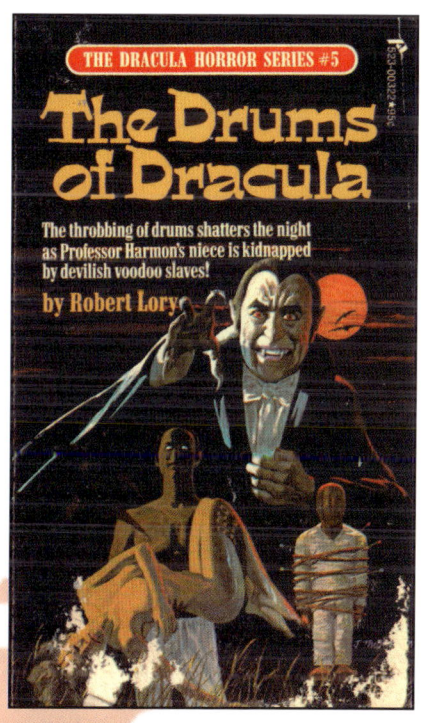

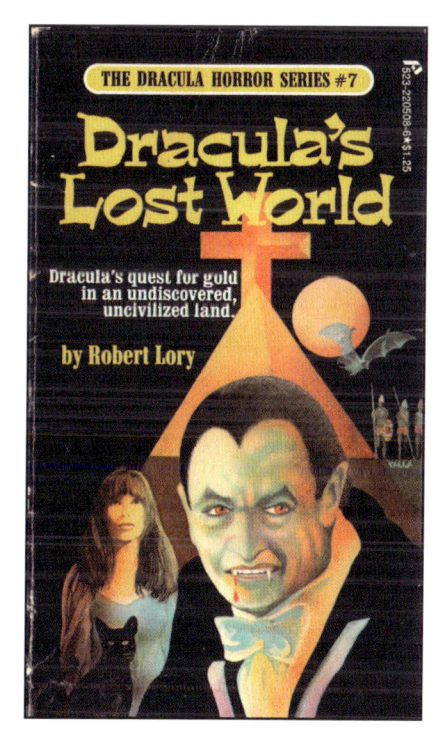

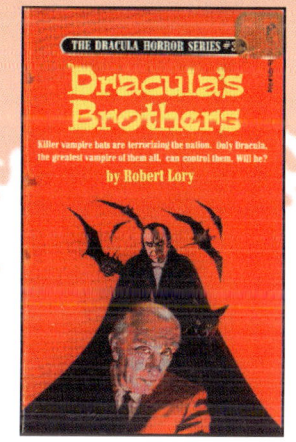

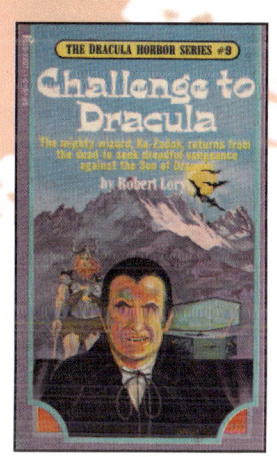

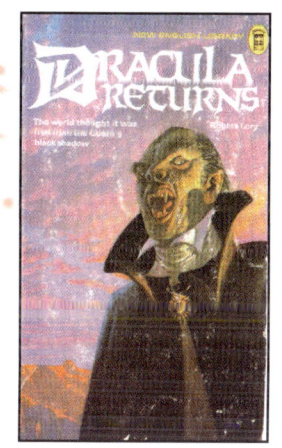

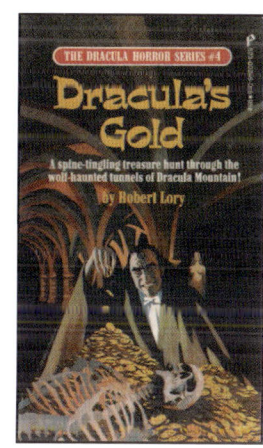

The Paperback Fanatic - Horror

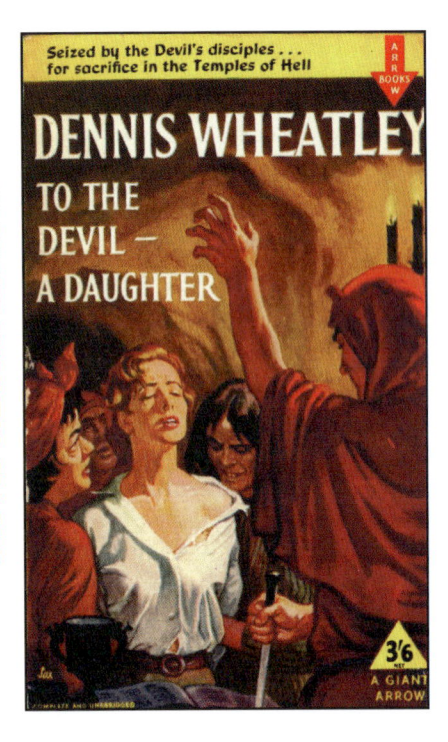

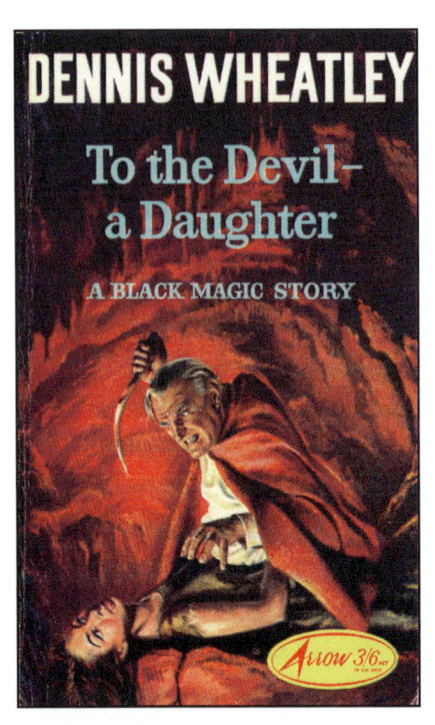

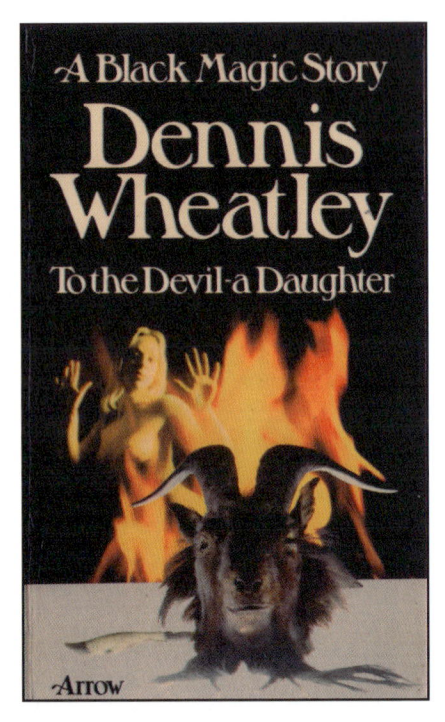

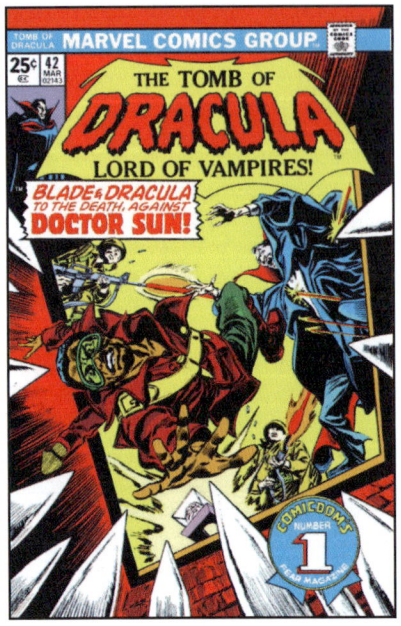

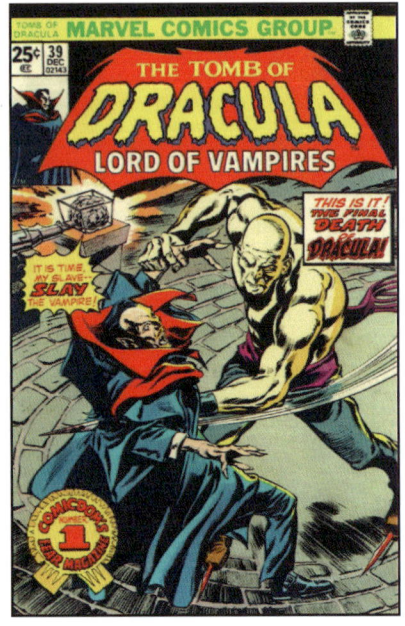

58

the horror seem almost plausible and grounded in reality. It does lead to a fair amount of exposition, though, which is probably a slight drawback for modern readers, but it does contribute to the atmosphere of believability that is so important for horror stories.

John Peel

movies, a TV series and an anime series. Welcome to some bloody good fun!

John Peel

THE TOMB OF DRACULA
Written (mostly) by Marv Wolfman
Illustrated by Gene Colan

"Each issue became a masterpiece of broody artwork..."

There have been, over the years, plenty of horror comics from **Tales from The Crypt** to **Vampirella** - but Marvel's **The Tomb of Dracula** is something else. Most of the comics tended to be short stories, generally with (supposedly) surprise, shock endings, but Dracula was different. Running for 70 issues starting in 1972, it continued the story of Bram Stoker's supernatural evil, and followed the fortunes of the well-known Lord of the Dead. Set in the then-modern day, it featured a band of vampire hunters, modern descendants of Van Helsing, Mina Harker and even a pre-vampiric Dracula himself, attempting to put a final stop to Dracula's activities. They (probably) succeeded in the final issue, but it's hard to keep a vampire down, isn't it? After a bit of a rocky start with the writers, things settled down with Marv Wolfman's long run on the comic, and all 70 issues were drawn by the ever-amazing Gene Colan, whose dynamic and cinematic style has never been better. Each issue became a masterpiece of broody artwork. Added to which, issue 9 saw the first story to feature another legendary character – Blade. This conflicted half-vampire was out to destroy all vampires – especially Dracula – with his trademark wooden throwing knives. Blade became remarkably popular and has (to date) been the subject of three

TWILIGHT EYES
Dean Koontz
1985

"Melding of science fiction, fantasy, thriller, and horror..."

The name Dean Koontz should be familiar to any modern reader of the horror genre. While he considers himself a "thriller" writer (who just happens to dabble into elements of the fantastic), there is no doubt his subject matter often treads the same roads as horror fiction. This is the case with such novels of his as *Phantoms*, *Darkfall* (AKA *Darkness Comes*), *77 Shadow Street*, and the **Odd Thomas** cycle. One perfect example of Koontz's melding of science fiction, fantasy, thriller, and horror can be found in *Twilight Eyes*. With so many books to his credit, this is often overlooked, but it definitely deserves some attention. The premise is the existence of genetically engineered beings which have lived in and around us for eons. They are "goblins," essentially, who feed off pain and suffering, and able to assume a human guise. Only a select few humans can see through these deceptions. One such person is Slim MacKenzie, who possesses "twilight eyes." Slim is a drifter, after having killed his uncle by marriage, who was a goblin responsible for several deaths in Slim's family. Want more? Slim joins a carnival as a way to travel the country while pursuing his personal vendetta against the goblins; so, you get a little taste of what carnival life was like in this period piece, as well. Enchanted Press published a particularly beautiful edition of *Twilight Eyes* in 1985, fully illustrated by Phil Parks. Koontz adopted a unique—and almost poetic—style which pairs well with the artwork of this edition. But, while it can still

---

THREE DAUGHTERS OF THE DEVIL Dennis Wheatley was hugely popular and constantly in print from the 1950s until the 1970s where his work seemingly disappeared overnight. Pictured are a 1956 edition with art by Sax, a 1964 edition with art by Sam Peffer, and a 1975 photo-cover edition.

THREE TOMBS FOR DRACULA Marvel Comics full-colour run of Dracula was unusual in that the same creative team of Marv Wolfman and Gene Colan persisted for the majority of the run, creating the most effective depiction of the vampire seen to date in the comics medium and a high-mark in comics.

be acquired affordably on the second-hand market, you'll still want to grab a 1987 or later (non-Enchanted Press) edition in order to read the story in its entirety. A bonus sequel story, of sorts, was added to subsequent releases. Overall, both editions are highly recommended reading for Koontz fans and all horror aficionados.
S. Clayton Rhodes

TWISTED TALES
Pacific Comics
1982-83
"Finally breaks with the slavish adherence to the EC formula..."

Heavily influenced by the famous 1950's EC Comics horror titles which consisted of 4 short stories of 6 pages with a shock ending, the ten issues of **Twisted Tales** haven't aged well. At the time, they were a revelation to teenage readers like me, as they bought the quality of artists perhaps associated with the undergrounds or **Heavy Metal** magazine into a comic that was formatted like a mainstream Marvel or DC title. Looking back now, beyond the sex and violence, many of the stories were not especially innovative compared with any of the vanilla DC mystery titles such as **The Unexpected** and **House of Mystery**, which were conforming to the restrictive Comics Code Authority guidelines. It did court some controversy with two stories: 'Banjo Lessons' in issue five which dealt with same-sex attraction and racism, and 'The Well' in issue four due to its full-frontal female nudity. John Bolton who illustrated 'The Well' and others, was the most impressive of the artists across the run, even considering the presence of the consistently superlative Richard Corben. My favourite stories were 'Speed Demons' in issue two about a ghostly and horny young couple who feel the need for speed, and 'Roomers' a melancholy tale which finally breaks with the EC formula that I feel restricted **Twisted Tales** artistic development. Another welcome development was adapting fiction works such as William F Nolan's 'The Party' and Dennis Etchison's 'Wet Season'. I think this was the most interesting aspect of the comic in retrospect and perhaps if it had continued in that direction, would have been a natural steppingstone for more intellectual horror such as the **Taboo** anthology series of the 1990s.
Justin Marriott

TWO FISTED ZOMBIES
Rick Veitch
1973
"Not counter-cultural enough to be an underground, but too off the wall for mainstream comics of that time..."

This was the fifth in a series of **All New Underground Comix** published by Last Gasp, intended to introduce creators who couldn't necessarily justify an ongoing title. Creator Rick Veitch was in his early 20s, the younger brother of Tom Veitch who would be the greatest writer in the underground comic movement collaborating with Richard Corben and most notably, Greg Irons. Rick Veitch would make his mark in mainstream comics with his work on **Swamp Thing** in the 1980s, although he fell afoul of a censorship move at that time. This is a very early work, a bizarre mix of superhero comic drawn in a Jack Kirby style, set in a post-apocalyptic world of zombies and warring factions, which I think he used as a portfolio to get into the Joe Kubert School of Cartooning. It was not counter-cultural enough to be an underground, but too off the wall for mainstream comics of that time. I enjoyed it greatly at the time, and it still has a crude power and offbeat nature that charms now, but many of the ideas and subjects have been consumed by the mainstream since then. A great curio-piece.
Justin Marriott

TWISTED TALES carried cover art by some of the giants of the genre. Richard Corben produced three of the images opposite, with his image of a startled night watchman discovering a dinosaur having a midnight snack a classic. Berni Wrightson's axe man with a belt of heads could have been carried on the cover of the infamous EC Comics of the 50s from which **Twisted Tales** chief writer Bruce Jones drew much inspiration. British artist John Bolton produced the other two covers displayed, with the illustration on issue four representing 'The Well', which based on the next issue's letters page, stirred up readers with its depiction of full frontal nudity. Jones argued it was essential to the story's twist. I read an interview with Bolton in which he stated he mutilated an action figure doll as photo reference for the man in the foreground.

The Paperback Fanatic - Horror

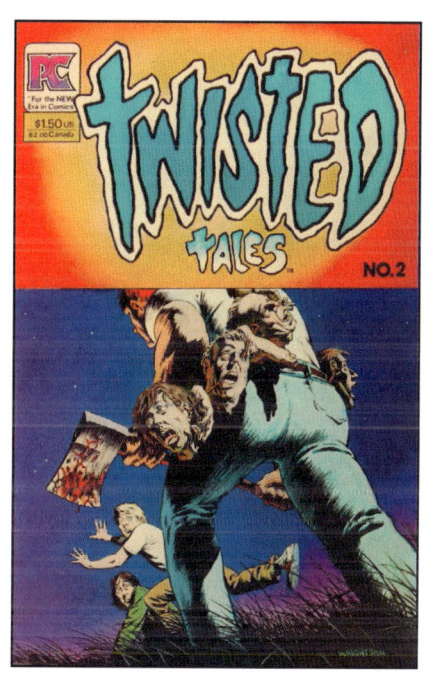

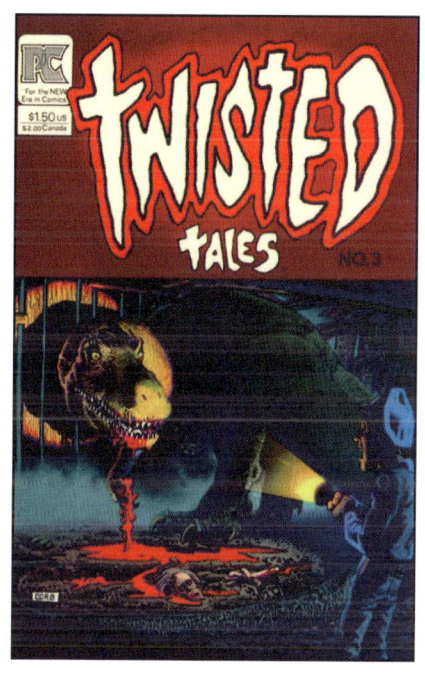

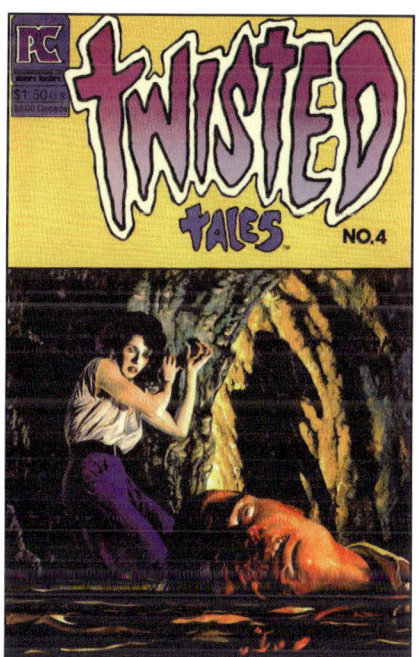

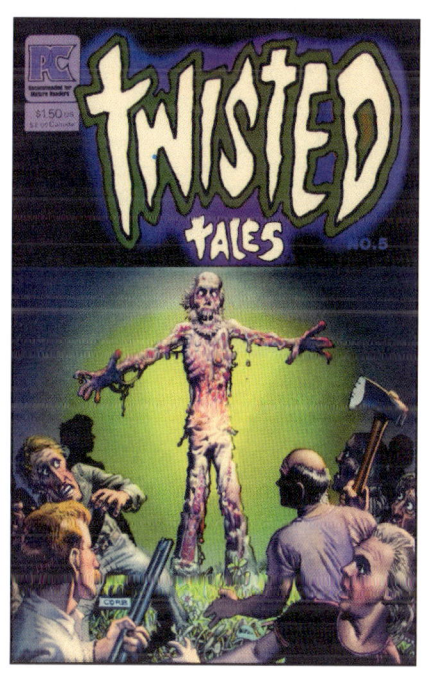

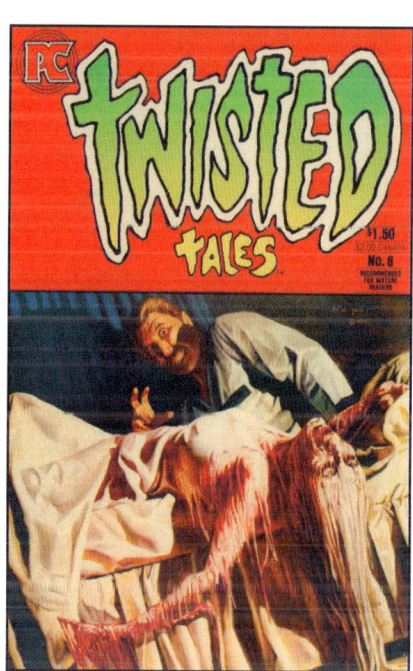

61

THE PAPERBACK FANTASTIC - HORROR

TWO THOUSAND MANIACS - THE COMIC
Malibu 1991
Written by Jack Herman
Illustrated by Tim Eldred

"You would be a maniac to spend any time or money on this..."

A three-issue mini-series which adapted the second in a trilogy of ground-breaking gore movies from H G Lewis intended for the Southern drive-ins of the 60s. In black and white, standard US comic size, this is a faithful enough adaptation of the movie. However, the charms of the movie could be argued as the low-budget gore effects, the cardboard chewing acting and the annoyingly catchy theme tune, none of which can be captured in a comic book. Indeed, the comic book depiction of the dismemberment and squishing is even less convincing than the impoverished special effects of the film, with the art from Tim Eldred noticeably deteriorating from a low starting point to looking as if the art for the final issue was run off in a weekend. Lewis had become something of a cult figure in the 90s and this was one of a number of publications intended to cash in on that, including a *Blood Feast* comic and reprints of the *Blood Feast* and *Two Thousand Maniacs* movie tie-in novels (yes, they do exist). You would be a maniac to spend any time or money on this.

Justin Marriott
☠

THE UNBIDDEN
Ronald Chetwynd-Hayes
1971

"A finale worthy of illustration by one of the grandmasters of horror comics..."

Chetwynd-Hayes was something of a divisive figure amongst British horror fans, and not widely known or published beyond British shores, due to his use of humour and conveyor belt of new monsters. However, this debut collection of short stories which appeared after some success with contributions to the **Pan Book of Horror Stories** which were written at the suggestion of his agent, was more hit than miss. House-bound horror was the dominant theme, with each tale unfolding between the four walls of suburban England, where the dwellings of the complacent and unsuspecting are invaded by the forces of evil. It doesn't get off to a great start, with 'No One Lived There' featuring an army of rats containing the minds of a cult of satanists, with a Lovecraft style climax. Better was 'The Devilet', which does manage to balance horror and humour when an obsessive hoarder purchases a black egg which soon hatches. In 'Come to me My Flower' RCH manages to makes the idea of flesh-eating bouquet believable and scary with excellent description and a finale worthy of one of horror comics grandmasters to have illustrated it. It included 'Gate Crasher', possibly RCH's most famous tale, an account of Jack the Ripper travelling through dimensions, which was part of the Amicus Films portmanteau *From Beyond the Grave*. There are enough straight-faced shockers in this collection to make me reconsider my dismissal of Chetwynd-Hayes as the Clown Prince of horror.

Justin Marriott
☠☠

THE UNHOLY SMILE
Gregory A. Douglas
1986

"A gothic romance on steroids..."

Gregory A. Douglas, author of the cult classic *The Nest*, was the pseudonym of Eli Cantor (1913-2006), who was born in New York, studied philosophy at New York University and received a law degree from Harvard University. *The Unholy Smile* is a gothic romance on steroids. Judith Bradford, a seventeen-year-old country girl who is escaping an abusive

---

2000 MANIACS During the late 1980s there was a boom in US independent comics, with Aircel one of the imprints that came and went. Like others of their ilk, the quality of their interiors were inferior to their painted covers.

THE UNBIDDEN Chris Achilleos painted this cover early in his career for Tandem, before finding recognition with a series of covers for tie-ins to the Dr Who TV series.

TWO FISTED ZOMBIES Although too mainstream for underground comics and too underground for mainstream comics, this post-apocalyptic zombie story contained ideas and images which since become commonly used in mainstream comics.

THE PAPERBACK FANTASTIC – HORROR

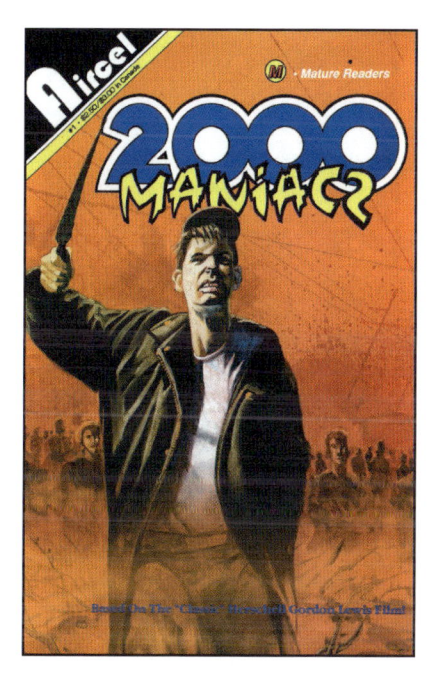

step father, arrives in New York to start a film career. She finds she has missed the rehearsal for a role in a Werner Christed film, who is a world-famous director. The location of the rehearsal, in a seedy part of Manhattan, is deserted except for a foreign couple, Lena and Gregor Ludovici, who work for Dr Felix Gomay, a rich man who is financing the film. Dr Gomay has a keen interest in sorcery and the occult and owns the island where the film is being made. Lena takes a shine to Judith and believes she has the looks Christed is after for his lead actress, so she convinces her husband to take Judith with them to Gomay Island in the hearse they use to transport film equipment around. At the island, Gregor and Lena feed a live rabbit to the guard dogs, and if that isn't enough of a shock, Judith finds that Dr Gomay's servants, whom he has brought over from Transylvania, all wear robes, cowls and masks, speak their own language and have their own religion. Judith falls in love with the handsome lead actor, Rick Gilbert, and in a series of 'accidents' that have led to the deaths of the two previous lead actresses, Judith find herself in the main female role. As it happens, Rick is in fact the great medieval serial killer and occultist Gilles de Rais, and Dr Gomay and Gregor are relatives and accomplices who are trying to raise the Devil in a Black Mass using a virgin sacrifice – the film is a ruse in which Werner Christed and his troupe are innocent players to play out the Black Mass. Additional plot threads are provided by Dr Gomay's homicidal daughter, Margot, who has murdered the two previous leads because she wants the role for herself, and Ursula Blake, a beautiful private detective who has been approached by Judith's mother to find her. Judith is variously attacked by the crazy daughter, drenched in goat's blood, almost raped by Gregor, before being saved by Werner Christed's state-of-the-art special effects equipment which uses holograph technology. The book would have been greatly improved if an editor had pruned it to half its 336 pages.
James Doig

VAMPIRE$
John Steakley
1990

"Like reading a hard-boiled men's adventure story..."

I really didn't know what to expect of this novel when I first began reading it and now that I've finished...I'm still not sure how I feel about it. It's the story of a group of mercenary vampire hunters who will clean out a nest in return for dollars. They don't really seem to do it for the pay though, so much as the idea of "somebody has to do it". The team is led by Jack Crow, who has been doing this for three years, which is longer than anybody else he's heard of. But he also knows he won't ever win the war; there will always be more nests and he and his team can't live forever. These vampires are tough creatures to kill. This is not Buffy's universe where you can simply go out on patrol, stake a few vamps here and there and call it a good night. These are horrendous monsters, and it takes all their ingenuity and teamwork just to kill the "normal" ones. When it comes to the masters, it's a whole 'nother level. Practically like fighting a deity. Parts of the novel were excellent, especially some of the fight scenes. My eyes were glued to the page to see how it would turn out. It's like reading a hard-boiled men's adventure story...with vampires. But other parts, unfortunately, were drawn out introspection or flashback descriptions of a character's past which I simply needed to plough through to hopefully get back to the good stuff again. The team members know their chances of living past the next battle are not good, so their down time is predictably crude and filled with hard drinking. Not especially fun to read about. Some of the characters are already broken, even at the beginning of the novel. The ending, as one might expect for this kind of novel isn't exactly uplifting but the vampire hunt will continue. It definitely reinforces the idea of "somebody has to do it."
Benjamin Thomas

THE UNHOLY SMILE Douglas' turbo-charged gothic only received solitary printings on either side of the Atlantic; Zebra US in 1981, and UK NEL in 1986 with a Stephen Crisp cover painting.

VAMPIRES Pictured is the 1990 edition. With the release of the John Carpenter directed adaptation, dropping the $ from the title and replacing with a S.

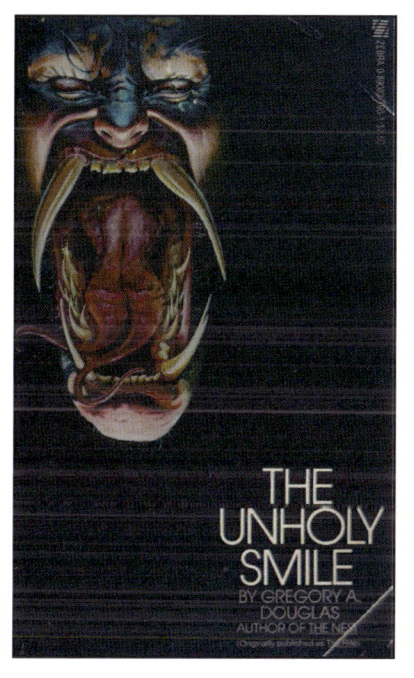

THE UNHOLY SMILE
By Gregory A. Douglas
Author of The Nest 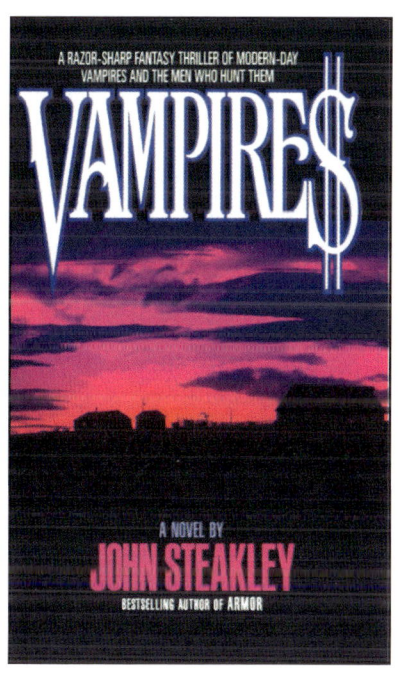
(Originally published as The Nest)

VAMPIRE$
A RAZOR-SHARP FANTASY THRILLER OF MODERN-DAY VAMPIRES AND THE MEN WHO HUNT THEM
A novel by JOHN STEAKLEY
Bestselling author of ARMOR

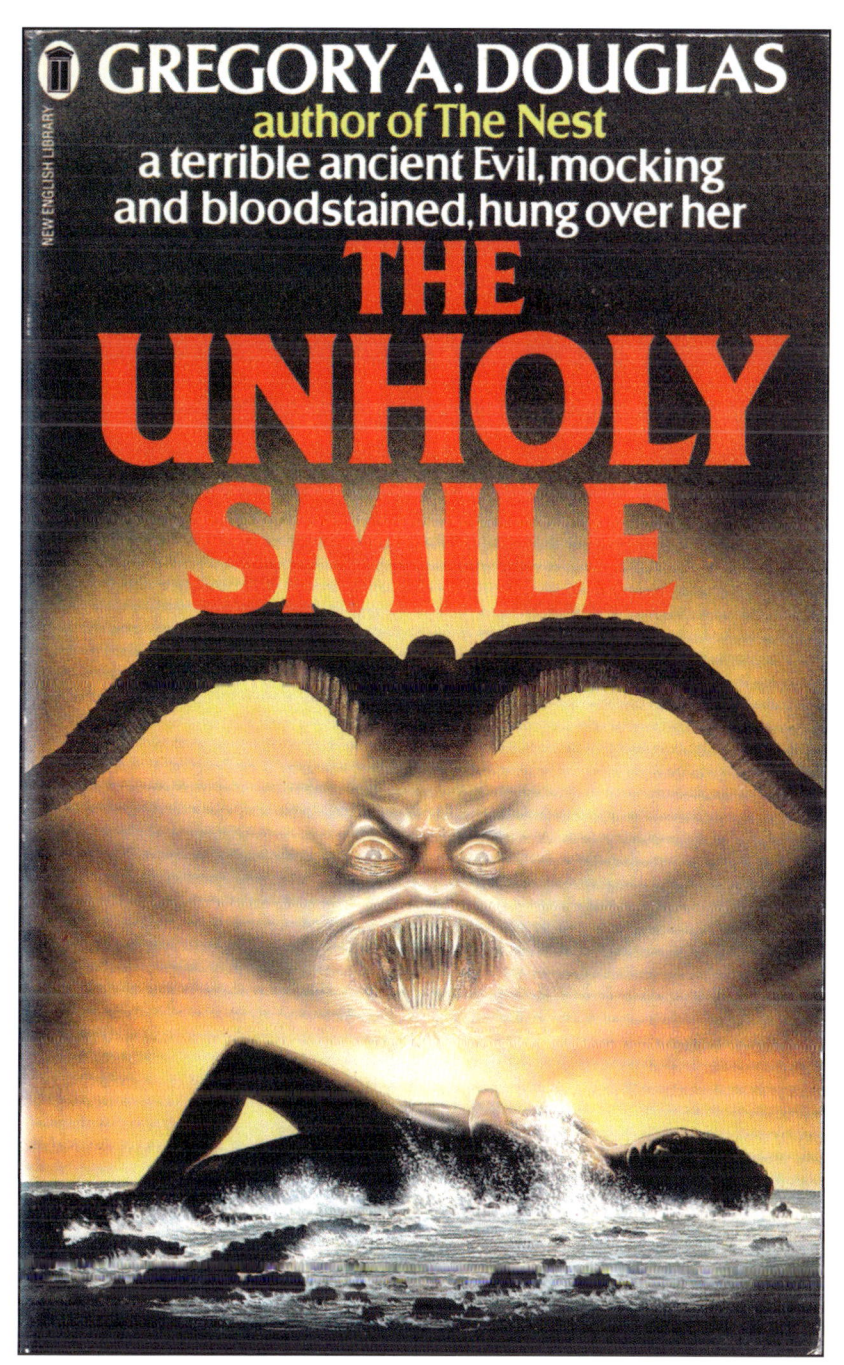

GREGORY A. DOUGLAS
author of The Nest
a terrible ancient Evil, mocking and bloodstained, hung over her
THE UNHOLY SMILE

The Paperback Fanatic — Horror

VILLAGE OF BLOOD
Ian Dear
1975

"Does boast one moment which left me slack-jawed..."

An anaemic read, which having telegraphed its denouement still takes an age to reveal all and most certainly doesn't spill enough of the crimson stuff. The people of Reston welcome a horror film crew into their midst but grisly events in their village begin to follow the film's script. Director Ken Mathers and investigative journalist Anne Green follow a trail that leads to the Lord Bellingham, mysterious financer of the film, whose ancestor had been burnt at the stake as a vampire by the people of Reston. Author Dear provides the occasional flash of inspiration, invoking flesh crawling revulsion when the wheel-chair-bound Bellingham is roused by a cut on Anne's hand and falls upon her in a slobbering frenzy, and dishes up the wonderful image of a meadow of gleaming white bones, the picked-clean remains of Bellingham's previous victims. It's just that he's too sparing with these sanguinary delights. Despite the obvious direction the story takes, it does boast one moment which left me slack-jawed; the village's elderly doctor bears many bite marks on his torso which the hero mistakenly assumes were the result of an unwanted vampire attack. He later realises they were in fact consensual love-bites applied by the vampire!
Justin Marriott
☠☠

THE VILLAGE OF FEAR
Martin Jenson
1974

"Reflects the real-life clash played out being the permissive society and self-appointed moral guardians..."

More of a macabre thriller than gothic horror, this is a story that lacks a sympathetic hero and any sense of tension, but is a compelling enough, and at times sleazy, portrait of a man fuelled by misguided religious fervour. Martin Trench is the vicar of a quintessentially British village (which no longer exist, if indeed they ever did), who sends three sanctimonious letters to members of his parish for the crimes of running a youth club which attracts bikers or a film society which shows continental art films. When all respond to Trench with sarcastic put-downs, Trench's mental health begins to deteriorate, and his clean-up mission turns into a vendetta of hammer bludgeoning, arson attacks and poisoning. Jenson strikes me as a skilled and witty author, and the book reflects the real-life clash played out being the permissive society and self-appointed moral guardians in the UK in the 1970s. Trench, who Jenson repeatedly skewers with droll humour, is presumably a stand-in for real-life morality campaigner Mary Whitehouse who had a high profile at the time, and his portrayal of Trench reminded me of elements of Dennis Potter's controversial play *Son of Man*, which portrayed Jesus as a mortal man plagued with doubts. Jenson's portrayal of women is not a flattering one, although one earthy woman eventually causes Trench to destroy himself. Needed to be more than just a criticism of misplaced morality and required some more sympathetic characters.
Justin Marriott
☠☠

WHISPERS
Stuart David Schiff
1987

"Niche but quality selection..."

This was a compilation drawn from the influential small press title of the same name, which ran to 24 issues from 1973 to 1984. Perhaps due to the support of high-profile professionals, **Whispers** consistently attracted top-notch contributors for the

---

VILLAGE OF FEAR Was packaged as No 2 in a 'Horror Series', which, like the Frankenstein Horror Series from Popular Library US, was a number of unconnected novels under a common banner. UK publisher NEL missed out a number, creating much anguish amongst completists.

VILLAGE OF BLOOD Another lurid and rough-hewn Ray Feibush cover for a lurid and rough-hewn early 70s NEL horror paperback.

WHISPERS Marshall Arisman brings some much needed class to this page with a clever and well executed image for this 1987 edition of an anthology drawn from Stuart David Schiff's small press mag.

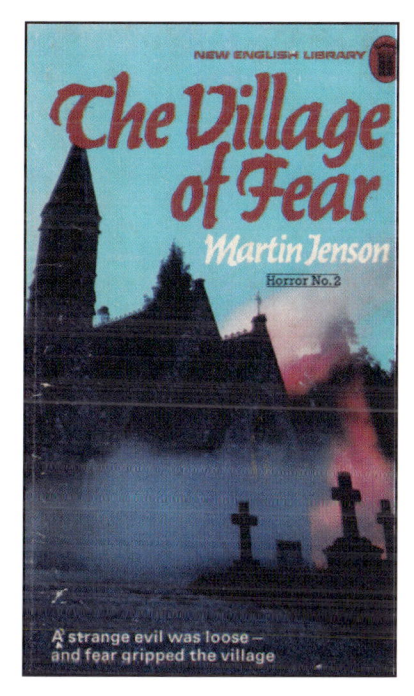

The Village of Fear
Martin Jenson
Horror No. 2

A strange evil was loose — and fear gripped the village

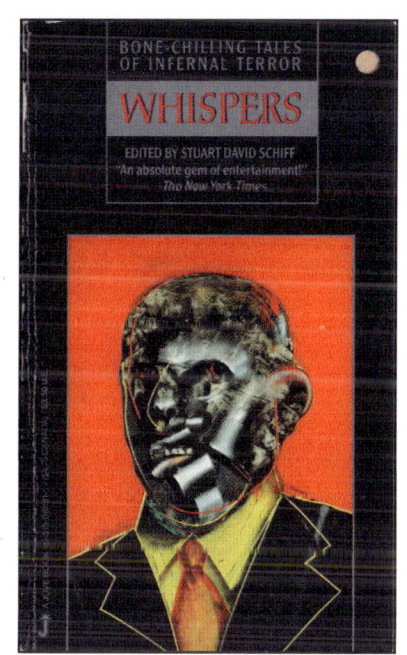

WHISPERS
BONE-CHILLING TALES OF INFERNAL TERROR
EDITED BY STUART DAVID SCHIFF
"An absolute gem of entertainment!" The New York Times

Village of Blood
Horror haunts the night
IAN DEAR

FANTASTIC FOCUS 7

DRAKULON LIVES!

VAMPIRELLA #2: ON ALIEN WINGS
Ron Goulart
1975

"Too much fun and flows too easily to be hack work..."

Vampirella was created by **Famous Monsters of Filmland's** own Forrest J. Ackerman and artist Trina Robinson. She's had a rocky fictional life and a rockier publication life, bouncing between publishers with multiple resets for the character story. Along the way Warner Books had the idea to get veteran pulpster Ron Goulart to write up some novels about the scantily clad alien-vampire who's actually a pretty nice lady. Apparently this six-book series pulls their stories directly from the comics written by Archie Goodwin. This would account for the episodic nature of *On Alien Wings* but Goulart's voice shines through even with someone else's ground work. He's a divisive kind of writer: personally I dig what he puts down while many others count him off as a hack. Nah, this book is too much fun and flows too easily to be hack work. How could you resist a book chock full of genetic werewolves, aquatic demons, a different demon cult, cruise ships staffed by zombies, drunken magicians, jokes, descendants of Van Helsing, and a spunky nearly nude alien/vampire woman? Goulart is a witty, clean writer and he makes this slim (seriously super-slim) volume fly by real easy. It's only slightly let down by the origins of the story. Perhaps if Goulart had come up with his own plot the book might have been smoother. Or maybe it's just better that Vampirella feels like a comic book even in novel form, because she's pure comic book stuff.

Roy Nugen

THE ENDURINGLY POPULAR ALIEN VAMPIRE FROM THE PLANET DRAKULON ORIGINALLY APPEARED IN WARREN MAGS AND THEN A PAPERBACK SERIES

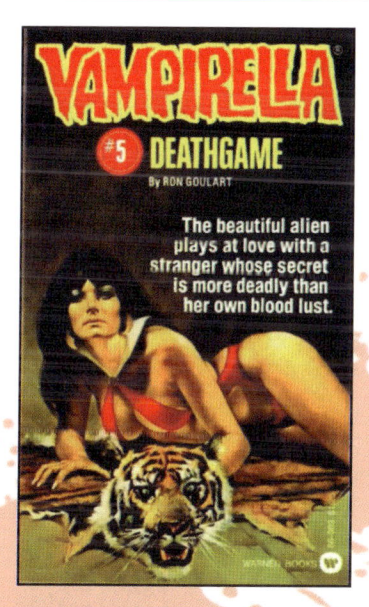

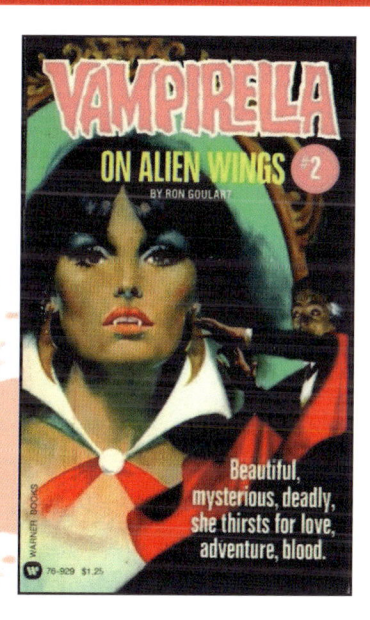

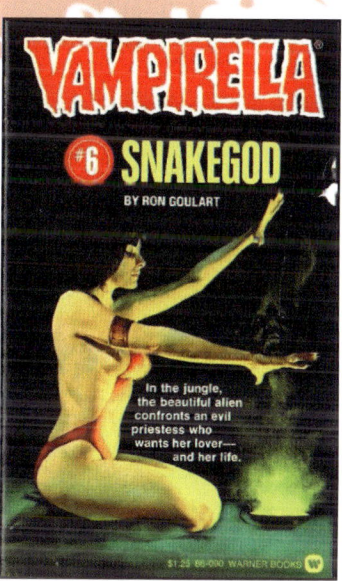

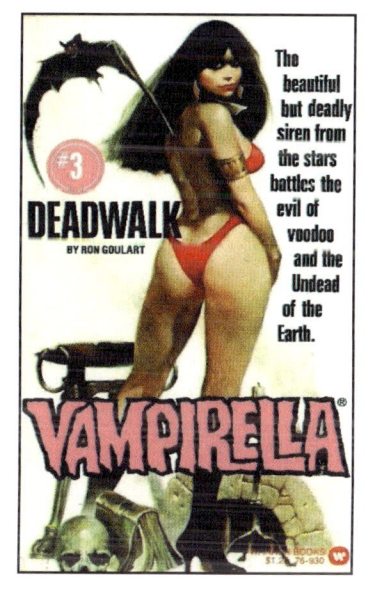

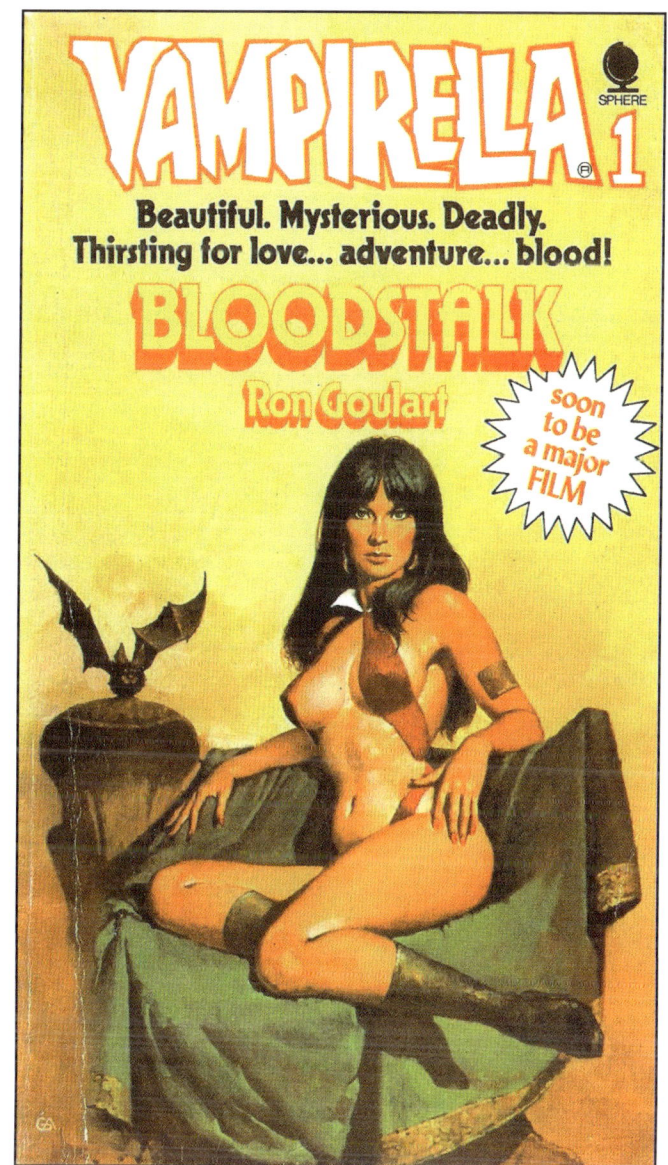

small-press, with this paperback containing Karl Edward Wagner, Dennis Etchison, Hugh Cave, Robert Bloch, Ray Russell, Ramsey Campbell and much more. As you might expect from a small-press publication, some material is aimed at hardcore fans, such as Robert Bloch's 'The Closer of the Way' in which the author has been banged up in an asylum and answers questions from a psychiatrist as to the contents of his books. 'Sticks' by Karl Edward Wagner is another example of this, inspired by the experience of artist Lee Brown Coyle and starring various small press figures, but it is a truly brilliant story. David Drake's 'The Barrow Troll' is a fantasy tale with a difference, which demands re-reading as well. I would imagine the readership of this volume are exactly the audience that would appreciate this niche but quality selection.

Justin Marriott

THE WRATH
David Robbins
1988

'Potential for tension later in the book is diffused by a repetitive emphasis on gun-porn...'

Those meddling nerds are at it again, this time an archaeologist who opens an Egyptian tomb and inadvertently unleashes a *28 Days Later* style virus which turns those infected into flesh-eating "dog-people". A combination of action-adventure with horror, the emphasis is on the former with flashes of morbid ingenuity. There is an especially effective early sequence in which an archaeologist seeks refuge in a sarcophagus which is besieged by the infected, but any further potential for tension later in the book is diffused by a repetitive emphasis on gun-porn. The rabid dog-people could easily be substituted by rabid terrorists or whomever America's bete noir of the time may have been, so it is little wonder that Robbins moved into men's adventure series writing with a degree of success.

Justin Marriott

ZACHERLEY'S MIDNIGHT SNACKS
ZACHARLEY'S VULTURE STEW
Both 1960

'Whomever pre-screened the pile had good taste...'

Two anthologies were attributed to Zacherley, a wise-cracking TV horror host on the East Coast of America who would become popular enough to put his name to novelty records and paperbacks. Who ghost-edited the first selection is lost in the sands of time, although I read a recollection from Zacherley of him reaching into a large pile of stories short-listed for him to read and just randomly picking whatever came to hand. Whomever pre-screened the pile had good taste as those lucky-dipped by Zacherley included Richard Matheson's delightfully creepy 'Sorry, Right Number', Jerome Bixby's and Joe Dean's seductive 'Share Alike' and the unsentimental 'The Whispering Gallery' by William F Temple. The rest of the package were made up of science-fiction writers such as A E Van Vogt and Henry Kuttner, and is not their best. That same year a follow-up appeared, and this time around Zacherley claimed to have read the story-pile and wanted to ensure it wasn't too graphic for younger readers who presumably were his core audience. They were certainly a more humorous selection than the other volume, such as the knowingly arch 'The Man Who Didn't Like Cats by L Ron Hubbard, which is not to my personal tastes. However, the overall quality is more consistent, such as James Blish's unconventional werewolf story 'There Shall be no Darkness'. Manly Wade Wellman's charming folk-horror 'The Devil is not Mocked' and the backwoods creep-a-thon 'They Bite'. With their lovely Richard Powers painted covers and the presence of cult figure Zacherley these are collected and priced beyond the ingenuity of their contents.

Justin Marriott

ZACHERLEY'S MIDNIGHT SNACKS
Richard Power's original art for the first of two anthologies published in 1960 as edited by TV horror host Zacherley.

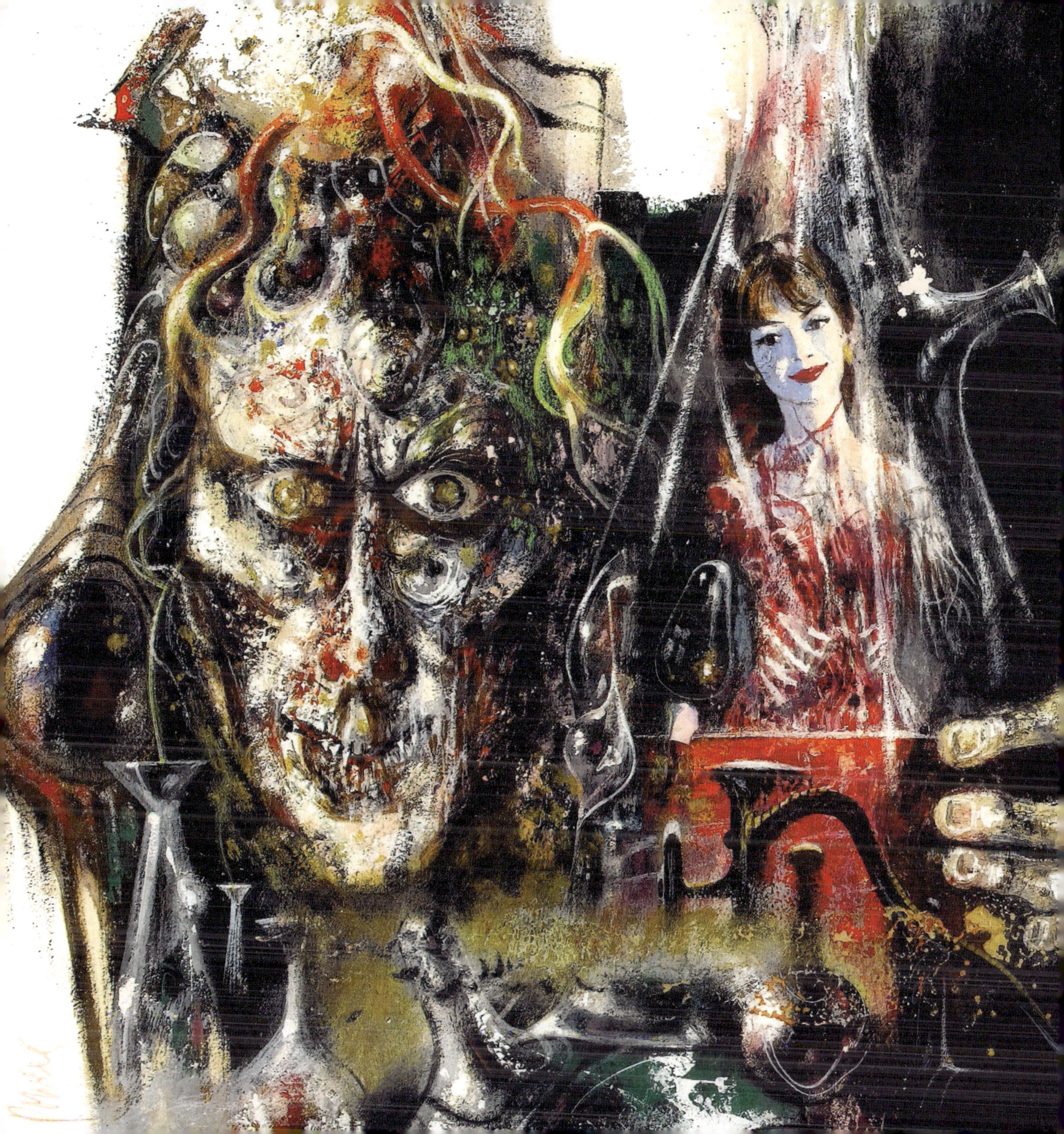

COLLECT ALL THREE ISSUES OF THE PAPERBACK FANTASTIC

SCIENCE FICTION!

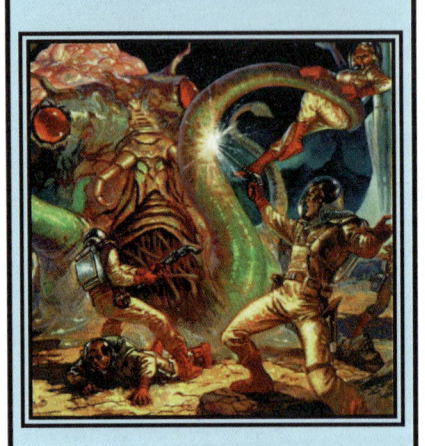

OUT NOW!

Reviews include Adam Strange, Adventures of Luther Arkwright, Alas Babylon, Armageddon 2419 AD, Atomic Knights, Barbarella, Bones of the Earth, Callahan's Crosstime Saloon, A Canticle for Leibowitz, Collision Course, The Day the Martians Came, Deathlok the Demolisher, The Destruction of the Temple, Dying of the Light, Essential Ellison, A Fighting Man of Mars, Flash Gordon, Fleshpots of Sansato, Footprints of Thunder, Frozen Hell, Gladiator-at-Law, The Glory That Was and more!

FANTASY!

OUT NOW!

Reviews include Elric, Red Sonja, Kane, Bran Mak Morn, Cormac Mac Art, Fafhrd & Gray Mouser, The Sword of Morningstar, Whetted Bronze, Brak the Barbarian, Kyrik, Wheel of Time, Brunner the Bounty Hunter, Savage Sword of Conan, Knight of Swords, Lord Foul's Bane, Volkhavaar, Spell of Seven, The Fantastic Swordsman, Blade, Slaine, Swords of Heaven, Flowers of Hell, Tales of Science and Sorcery, Nemesis the Warlock, Mythago Wood, Solomon Kane, Tarzan and more!

HORROR!

OUT NOW!

Reviews include The Ants, The Apocalypse, Books of Blood, Children of the Night, The Conjurers, The Degenerates, Devil Daddy, Draco the Dragon Man, The Evil Under the Water, Headhunter, Homunculus, Killer Crabs, An Odour of Decay, Manstopper, Nightshades and Damnations, The Offspring, Sabat, The Saxonbury Machine, The Slime Beast, Tapping the Vein, Twisted Tales, Two Thousand Maniacs, Village of Blood, Whispers, The Wrath, Zacharley's Vulture Stew and more!

Printed in Great Britain
by Amazon